S0-BBK-534

DARRINGTON
Ranger District

DARRINGTON
RANGER DISTRICT

The Darrington Ranger District would like to thank all of the individuals and groups who have volunteered and continue to volunteer their time and effort to help maintain our district trails. We invite others to join the effort. Please contact our district office for more details.

IMPORTANT PHONE NUMBERS

Emergency **911**

Mountain Pass Report

Dial **511** or

1-800-695-7623

Avalanche Conditions

1-206-526-6677

Forest Fires (USFS local)

1-800-826-3383

Forest Fires (State DNR)

1-800-562-6010

National Weather Service

http://nimbo.wrh.noaa.gov/

Copyright © 2009 Discover Your Northwest

All rights reserved. No part of this publication may be reproduced or transmitted in any form or by any means, electronic or mechanical, including photocopy, recording, or any information storage and retrieval system, without permission in writing from the publisher.

All interior photographs generously provided by Gary Paull

All content made possible with invaluable assistance from the USDA Forest Service Staff at Darrington Ranger District, Mt. Baker-Snoqualmie National Forest.

Design: Mark MacKay
      Ben Nechanicky

Editorial Assistant: Suzanne Greninger

Printed in United States of America

Published in the United States of America by Discover Your Northwest, a 501(c)(3) non-profit organization.

ISBN: 0-914019-47-3

978-0-914019-47-3

MOUNT BAKER-SNOQUALMIE NATIONAL FOREST
Ranger Districts

Darrington Ranger District
1405 Emens Avenue N.
Darrington, WA 98241
360-436-1155

Verlot Public Service Center
33515 Mtn. Loop Highway
Granite Falls, WA 98252
360-691-7791

Mt. Baker Ranger District
810 State Route 20
Sedro-Woolley, WA 98284
360-856-5700

Glacier Public Services Center
Glacier, WA 98244
360-599-2714

Heather Meadows Visitor Center
Milepost 556, State Route 542
Glacier, WA 98244
360-856-5700

Skykomish Ranger District
74920 NE Stevens Pass Hwy.
Skykomish, WA 98288
360-677-2414

**Snoqualmie Ranger District
North Bend Office**
902 SE North Bend Way
North Bend, WA 98045
425-888-1421

**Snoqualmie Ranger District
Enumclaw Office**
450 Roosevelt Ave. E
Enumclaw, WA 98022
360-825-6585

**Mt. Baker-Snoqualmie
National Forest Supervisor's Office**
2930 Wetmore Avenue, Suite 3A
Everett, WA 98201
425-783-6000
TTY 425-783-0127
800-627-0062
http://www.fs.fed.us/r6/mbs

Outdoor Recreation Information Center
Seattle REI Building
222 Yale Avenue North
Seattle, WA 98109
206-470-4060

COVER PHOTO: Glacier Peak and Whitechuck River Valley © Gary Paull

DARRINGTON
Ranger District

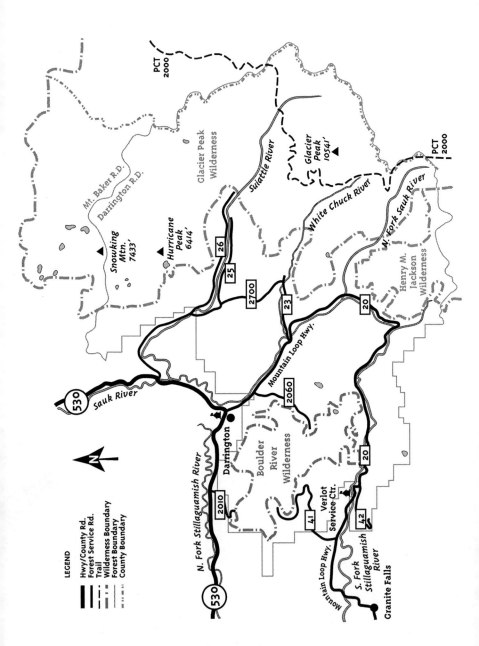

Maps in this trail guide are for general orientation only and are not to scale. Please use a USDA Forest Service or other detailed topographic map for accurate and specific information.

INTRODUCTION

The Darrington Ranger District is located about 30 miles east from Interstate 5 along the Mountain Loop Highway off State Route 530. Half of this remarkable 570,000-acre area is congressionally designated as the following three Wilderness areas: Boulder River, Henry M. Jackson, and Glacier Peak. The latter two areas are jointly administered by the Skykomish Ranger District and the Okanogan-Wenatchee National Forest.

From Darrington, drive the Mountain Loop Highway to the southern part of the District. There you can discover Verlot Public Service Center, near the South Fork Stillaguamish River. Constructed by the Civilian Conservation Corps (CCC) from 1933 to 1942, Verlot's handsome buildings reflect both the architectural style and fine craftsmanship of that era and are listed on the National Register of Historic Places. Operating seasonally, the center's staff will help you plan your outing and provide you with good directions and up-to-date conditions.

Leave No Trace and Tread Lightly

Increasing numbers of visits and visitors make it more important than ever that all user groups travel and camp with minimum impacts on the land and its resources. You can help preserve your National Forest lands and the quality of your outdoor experience by following these important guidelines and regulations:

Pack it Out If you pack it in you are required to pack it out. Take a trash bag and pack out all litter. In areas where fires are allowed please remember a fire ring is not a trash receptacle; do not leave your litter for others to burn as it merely attracts animals, particularly mice and sometimes bears, to campsites.

Human Waste Use toilets when provided, otherwise be sure to bury it. The top 6 or 8 inches of soil has a system of "biological disposers" that work to decompose organic material. Use a small digging tool and bury waste in a hole 6 to 8 inches deep, at least 200 feet from water, trails, and campsites.

Keep the top layer of sod intact and replace it when done. Exposed human waste is a health hazard and an eyesore. Where digging is not possible, such as in subalpine areas, snow, rock, or glacier, pack it out.

Stay on the Trail Cutting switchbacks destroys vegetation, ruins the trail, and causes erosion. When stopping for a break or to eat lunch, try to stay on resilient areas such as the trail itself or on rocky areas and logs where you will do little damage to plants and soil.

Camp in Established Spots Whenever possible, use existing sites 200 feet from lakeshores. It prevents impacts on undamaged areas and helps protect fragile lakeshores and water quality. Camp in a well drained spot so you can avoid digging trenches around your tent.

Preserve the Quiet Try to camp away from other parties and avoid loud shouting, singing, or playing music at high volume.

Use Camping Stoves Even in areas outside no campfire zones, firewood is getting scarce. Please use stoves for cooking and if you have a campfire, make it a small one in an existing fire ring. Use only dead or down wood and always make sure your fire is out before leaving camp. It is hazardous and illegal to leave a campfire unattended.

Off Trail Travel Travel in small groups if you leave the trail. Remember to avoid fragile areas and spread out—don't follow the same route.

Stock Users Keep your stock at least 200 feet from lakes except when watering animals or traveling on established trails. Use lightweight equipment and pack lightly. Use a high hitch line when tying stock and set it up well away from camps, trails, and streams (tying stock to trees can cause massive damage to trees and the plants and soils around them). When grazing stock, use hobbles or lightweight electric fence systems. When you break camp, scatter the horse manure and leave the site in as good or better shape than when you found it. Resist the temptation to cut switchbacks.

Preserve Water Quality When washing dishes, bathing, or brushing your teeth, collect water in a pot or basin and carry it 200 feet away from water sources before using it. After washing, bury dirty water and toothpaste in a hole 4-6 inches deep.

Trail Etiquette

With the increasing number and variety of users on many of the forest trails, it is important that we all practice the following:

Hikers Whenever necessary, hikers (because of their greater mobility) should yield the right of way to horse or stock users, move to the downhill side of the trail, make no sudden movements, and speak normally to the animals and/or their riders so that the animals will know you are not a threat.

Respect Wildlife Watch wildlife from a distance and keep pets from harassing wild animals.

Stock Users When approaching hikers, be courteous and advise them on the best way to avoid spooking your animals.

Mountain Bikers When encountering stock, dismount and move yourself and your bike to the downhill side of the trail. Speak in a normal tone of voice to reassure the animals. Remember that bicycles are quiet and therefore give little warning of their approach, so ride cautiously. Expect to encounter others at any time and place on the trails.

Dogs must be leashed or under voice command.

Safety and Security Considerations

Everyone should be aware of the risks involved in venturing out onto the trails. Weather can change quickly and drastically. Trail conditions can vary depending on location, maintenance level, and weather influences. Hazards are not signed. One's own levels of experience, knowledge, and physical condition are safety factors also. Each user is responsible for his or her own safety and should be prepared and alert for unexpected events and conditions. A variety of books and pamphlets on outdoor preparedness, safety, and survival are available in bookstores, outdoor equipment stores, and government offices.

Before you head out, listen to weather forecasts and contact the ranger station for current trail conditions. Let someone know where you are going and when you will return.

The increasing popularity of trail recreation has brought with it a corresponding increase in thefts from unattended vehicles at trailheads. It is recommended that you don't leave valuable, easily carried items in your vehicle (such as cameras, CD and MP3 players, wallets, etc.) and don't tell strangers at the trailhead your destination or duration of trip. If you see something suspicious, report it as soon as possible to the nearest law enforcement agency or Forest Service employee.

Essential Survival Items

ALWAYS let someone know the proposed route you are taking and what time you plan to return. Remember: If you get lost, find a tree or log and stay put. Make sure the following items are in your pack before leaving:

▶ Extra clothing, including rain gear

▶ Extra food

▶ Sun glasses

▶ Knife (pocketknife will do)

▶ Matches (in waterproof container)

▶ Fire starter (waxed paper, candle, other)

▶ First aid kit

▶ Flashlight with fresh batteries

▶ Map

▶ Compass

▶ Whistle

Water Quality

Because of the spread of the parasite *giardia* in recent years, it is recommended that all water be boiled, filtered, or treated before drinking, particularly in heavy use areas.
Information on *giardia* and methods to prevent it is available in outdoor sport stores, guide books, magazine articles, and from your doctor.

Campfires

It is hazardous and illegal to leave a campfire unattended. See individual trail listings for specific campfire restrictions. This region frequently experiences high fire danger during late summer, campfires may be completely prohibited during these times. For up-to-date information, contact the closest Ranger District office for current conditions and restrictions.

Horse Sense

The Darrington Ranger District trail system has much to offer the trail rider. Short day trips or long excursions are possible on the district's 173 miles of stock trail.

Much of the backcountry of the wilderness areas are in the fragile, high-elevation uplands where soil is thin, plant cover easily disturbed, and forage is limited. Good horse handling techniques and backcountry manners minimize damage to the forest.

Avoid animal pollution of water by tying, picketing, and grazing pack and saddle stock in areas away from water sources. Please do not tie stock directly to trees. Use a highline, hobble or picket your animals. Do not let stock overgraze fragile alpine areas. We recommend bringing feed. On national forest lands all feed must be commercially processed pellets, steamed or rolled grains, or state-certified weed-free feed. Good stock handlers keep the backcountry as they found it and take pride in leaving little evidence that they and their animals were there.

There are several stock facilities and stock camps scattered throughout the district. These facilities are located at the Suiattle River trailhead, North Fork Sauk trailhead, and the Bald Eagle trailhead.

Please keep in mind that a moderate stock trail in the mountains can still be a difficult trail. Most trails on the Darrington Ranger District have steep side slopes and sometimes narrow tread. Please make sure your animals are in shape and experienced for mountain travel. Expect the unexpected. Even if a trail has been recentl-y maintained, trees or rocks can fall and unexpectedly block the trail way.

Northwest Forest Pass

A Northwest Forest Pass, or other honored pass, is required for parking at most trailheads. Revenue from Northwest Forest Pass sales goes directly to trails and trailhead maintenance. Passes can be purchased at any Forest Service office, many outdoor stores, and on the internet at www.discovernw.org. You can purchase a day pass or annual pass and they are good for parking at any National Forest trailhead in Oregon and Washington as well as many other recreation sites. A pass is required for each vehicle regardless of number of passengers. For further information, contact any Forest Service office or visit www.discovernw.org.

Wilderness Regulations

Many of the trails in the Darrington Ranger District are partly or entirely within designated wilderness boundaries. In order to protect wilderness resources and provide you and others with quality wilderness experiences, the following regulations are in effect for all wilderness areas:

▶ Obey all fire closures.

▶ Group size is limited to twelve heartbeats; this includes any combination of people, livestock, or pets.

▶ Use of motorized or mechanized equipment is prohibited. This restriction includes bicycles and hangliders.

▶ Caching, leaving, or storing equipment, personal property, or supplies unattended for more than 48 hours is prohibited.

▶ Use commerciallly processed pellets, steamed or rolled grains, or state-certified weed-free for livestock. Unprocessed feed is prohibited, it introduces undesireable non-native plant species into wilderness environments.

▶ Grazing any pack or saddle animal within 200' of any shoreline is prohibited. Do not hitch, tether, or hobble any pack or saddle animal within 200' of any shoreline.

▶ No cutting allowed. Cutting standing trees, snags, or boughs is prohibited. Healthy trees and decrepit snags are beautiful and necessary components of a healthy ecosystem.

Trail Guide Symbols

The following symbols are used throughout this guide to indicate which trails are open to which kind of use.

🚶 Hikers Permitted on Trail   🐴 Horses and Other Stock Permitted

🚲 Bicycles Permitted on Trail   ♿ Barrier Free Trail

Difficulty Symbols

The following symbols will be used to designate the degree of difficulty a hiker in average physical condition may encounter on the trail. This difficulty rating is determined by trail condition and route location factors such as steepness of grade, elevation changes, availability of drinking water, obstacles, and harshness of terrain. Snow, ice, rain, and other weather conditions may increase the levels of difficulty.

Moderate:
Users require
limited skill
and encounter
few challenges.

More Difficult:
Users require
some skill and
experience more
challenging terrain.

Most Difficult:
Users require a high
degree of skill
and experience
challenging travel.

DISCLAIMER

Safety is a major concern for all outdoor activities. Outdoor activities carry some unavoidable risks that everyone needs to understand and respect. The fact that a trail is described in this publication does not mean that it is safe for you. A trail that is safe for an experienced, well-equipped hiker in good physical condition on a warm, dry day may be dangerous for a less experienced or poorly equipped person or on a rainy, foggy, cold, or stormy day. Weather and trail conditions can change, sometimes with little warning. Minimize risks before your hike:

▶ Check local weather and trail conditions before you begin

▶ Tell someone where you're going and when you will be back

▶ Sign in at all trailheads and speak with the local ranger whenever possible

▶ Be alert, prepared, and adequately equipped when in the backcountry

▶ Know your own capabilities, experience, and limitations

▶ If conditions are dangerous, or if you are not prepared to deal with them safely, choose a different activity

The authors and publisher assume no responsibility for the outcome of any activities included in this book. Although we have tried to be accurate, roads, trails, and other conditions cannot be predicted and may have changed since the information was compiled. You are responsible for your own actions. Authors and publisher disclaim liability for any loss or injury arising out of the use of the information in this publication.

NON-WILDERNESS AREAS

With over three hundred miles of trail to choose from throughout the district, recreational opportunities are endless. Many trails meander along creeks and streams, which provide cool spots for fishing or picnicking. Others lead to spectacular views of the valley below.

These non-wilderness trails exist for people of all abilities; some are relatively flat and wander through old-growth forests or popular wildlife areas. For the hardier hikers and stock users, many routes lead into alpine meadows with clear lakes surrounded by mountain peaks.

Theft at parking areas is an increasing problem. Leave all valuables at home. Items left in the trunk of your car are not safe. If you are a victim of "car clouting," report it to the nearest ranger station or call the County Sheriff's Office.

If the trail crew has not preceded your visit, be prepared for windfalls across the trail and brushy conditions. Most of the main trails are generally maintained by late July or early August, depending on snow melt and winter storm damage. Check with the Darrington or Verlot Ranger Station for current trail conditions before you head out.

ASHLAND LAKES TRAIL DNR

Washington State Department of Natural Resources

LENGTH: 4.2 miles **BEST SEASONS:** summer, fall
LOW ELEVATION: 2200 ft. **HIGH:** 3000 ft. **GAIN:** 800 ft.

TRAILHEAD ACCESS: From the Verlot Public Service Center, travel east on the Mtn. Loop Highway for 4.5 miles. Turn right on the Schweitzer Creek Road 4020. Continue 2.3 miles to the Bear Lake Road 4021 and follow it for 1.5 miles to a junction with an obvious spur road on the left. Turn left and follow this road to the trailhead parking area.

PARKING AND FACILITIES: Limited parking and ADA toilet facilities available.

DESCRIPTION: The Ashland Lakes are within the Morning Star Natural Resources Conservation Area (NRCA). This NRCA is managed by the Washington State Department of Natural Resources primarily to protect high-quality wetlands, fragile subalpine meadows, sensitive plant communities, and habitat for threatened, endangered, and rare wildlife species. Opportunities for low-impact public use are allowed if they do not adversely affect ecological processes and are currently provided with the Ashland Lakes Trail leading to four primitive backcountry camps.

The trail follows an old roadbed for the first mile through a stand of young trees before entering an old-growth hemlock forest. At approximately 1.7 miles a junction is reached. The left fork leads to Beaver Plant Lake, a sensitive wetland of sphagnum bog and peat. The right fork continues past the junction with the Bald Mountain Trail to Upper Ashland Lake and Lower Ashland Lake—larger and deeper lakes at the headwaters of Wilson Creek. Continuing on the trail, past Ashland Lakes, the trail becomes very difficult and is not recommended for inexperienced hikers or children. The trail eventually ends at Twin Falls Lake. Use caution in this area of dangerous cliffs and observe the marked barriers.

The campsites are located near these lakes. Please stay on the boardwalks to protect the sensitive shoreline vegetation and camp in designated sites only. There are no toilet facilities at the camps. Use "Leave No Trace" methods. Use caution on the boardwalks, which can be slippery when wet.

For more information about the NRCA, contact the DNR at 360-856-3500.

NON-WILDERNESS TRAILS

BALD MOUNTAIN TRAIL
Washington State Department of Natural Resources

**LENGTH: 10.7 miles BEST SEASONS: summer, fall
LOW ELEVATION: 2600 ft. HIGH: 4500 ft. GAIN: 1900 ft.**

TRAILHEAD ACCESS: From the Verlot Public Service Center, drive east on the Mtn. Loop Highway 4.5 miles to the Schweitzer Creek Road 4020. Turn right and follow this road for 2.3 miles to Bear Lake Road 4021. Turn right and continue 1.5 miles to a junction with an obvious spur road on the left. Turn left and follow this road to the Ashland Lakes trailhead parking area.

PARKING AND FACILITIES: Limited parking and ADA toilet facilities available.

DESCRIPTION: The Bald Mountain Trail is within the Morning Star Natural Resources Conservation Area (NRCA). This NRCA is managed by the Washington State Department of Natural Resources. Opportunities for low-impact public use are allowed if they do not adversely affect ecological processes and are provided by this primitive trail, which traverses the crest of Bald Mountain Ridge between the Ashland Lakes and Cutthroat Lakes. Access to the Bald Mountain Trail is from the Ashland Lakes Trail, just past Beaver Plant Lake. Views of Three Fingers, Whitehorse, Mt. Pilchuck, Spada Lake, and the valleys below are to be found along the trail. This trail can be difficult to follow as it passes through open forest and talus slopes along the ridge.

Primitive backcountry camps are available at the lakes, but there are no campsites and very little water in between. There are no toilet facilities at the camps. Cutthroat Lakes Camp is in a NO CAMPFIRE zone. Campers should bring a stove and use "Leave No Trace" methods.

For more information about the NRCA, contact the DNR at 360-856-3500.

BARLOW POINT TRAIL 709

**LENGTH: 1.2 miles BEST SEASONS: summer, fall
LOW ELEVATION: 2360 ft. HIGH: 3200 GAIN: 840**

TRAILHEAD ACCESS: From the Verlot Public Service Center, travel east on the Mtn. Loop Highway 19.4 miles to the trailhead at Barlow Pass.

PARKING AND FACILITIES: There is a parking lot and toilet facilities at the Barlow Pass trailhead.

DESCRIPTION: The trail begins at the site of the old Barlow Pass Guard Station and at 0.3 mile, encounters a junction. The left branch leads to Old Government Trail 733. The main trail skirts the foot of a large outcrop of volcanic rock. A series of gentle switchbacks leads to the crest of the ridge, which burned in the Buck Creek fire early in the century. At 1.1 miles the summit is reached at the site of the Barlow Point Lookout, which has excellent views of the South Fork Sauk and South Fork Stillaguamish Valleys. Drinking water is not available along this trail.

BEAR LAKE TRAIL 661

LENGTH: 0.3 mile   BEST SEASONS: summer, fall
LOW ELEVATION: 2650 ft.   HIGH: 2775 ft.   GAIN: 125 ft.

TRAILHEAD ACCESS: From the Verlot Public Service Center, travel east on the Mtn. Loop Highway 4.5 miles. Turn right (south) on Schweitzer Creek Road 4020 and continue 2.3 miles to Bear Lake Road 4021. Turn right onto this road and continue for 3.4 miles to the trailhead.

PARKING AND FACILITIES: Limited parking. No toilet facilities at trailhead.

DESCRIPTION: Because it is a short hike from the road, this popular lake is a good destination for beginning backpackers. The lake is entirely surrounded by forest and although it is 30 feet deep, it offers only fair fishing for the angler. The 2.1-mile-long trail to Pinnacle Lake is an attraction for day hikers. A backcountry toilet is provided on the hillside above the north shore of the lake. Please use this facility for its intended purpose and not for trash disposal. The Bear Lake area has suffered from the effects of heavy use over the years. You can help by:

1. Camping at least 100 feet away from the shore.

2. Using a backpacking stove since firewood is scarce and cutting live trees is prohibited.

BEAVER LAKE TRAIL 783

LENGTH: 0.5 miles   BEST SEASONS: spring, summer, fall
LOW ELEVATION: 900 ft.   HIGH: 1000 ft.   GAIN: 100 ft.

TRAILHEAD ACCESS: From the Darrington Ranger Station, take the Mtn. Loop Hwy. 20 along the west side of the Sauk River. Follow this road 10 miles, going past the Sauk River crossing. Just past the bridge (on the right) is the road to the trailhead. The road is 0.2 mile in length and is signed.

PARKING AND FACILITIES: There is a parking lot at the trailhead. No toilet facilities.

DESCRIPTION: This trail is an easy hike designed to provide a view of beavers at work, or just a chance to enjoy the serenity of the river and forest. The entire trail follows an old railroad grade—watch for the last of the decaying trestles along the way. The trail ends at the river where the trail was washed out during high waters in 2006. When reaching this point, a view of Pugh Mountain can be enjoyed on a clear day. This trail gets shorter by the year; the beaver ponds for which the trail was named are no longer accessible.

BIG FOUR ICE CAVES TRAIL 723

**LENGTH: 1.25 miles   BEST SEASONS: spring, summer, fall, winter
LOW ELEVATION: 1700 ft.   HIGH: 1900 ft.   GAIN: 200 ft.**

TRAILHEAD ACCESS: From the Verlot Public Service Center, go east on the Mtn. Loop Highway 14.5 miles to the Big Four Picnic Area.

PARKING AND FACILITIES: Picnic area with tables and fire grates, toilets, parking area with room for buses and trailers. No camping is allowed at Big Four.

DESCRIPTION: A new trailhead has been built approximately 0.25 mile up the road from the existing trailhead. A 0.25 mile interpretive and barrier free trail connects the two. Picnic facilities are located at the old trailhead (Big Four Picnic Area). The trailhead has ample room for cars, buses, and trailers.The route from the picnic area begins on the same concrete walks used during the Big Four Inn's heyday. Elevated boardwalks cross a low, marshy area created by active beavers. Just before the South Fork Stillaguamish River the trail loops back to connect with the new parking area and eventually with the picnic area creating a 0.75-mile loop. The main trail continues through the woods on a footbridge over the South Fork of the Stillaguamish River. This portion of the trail is more difficult.

The trail enters a dense forest, and just beyond it are the first close-up views of the ice fields and the immense north face of the 6153 ft. Big Four Mountain. The caves are usually exposed during August and remain visible through October since they are melt outlet openings at the base of a permanent snowfield.

WARNING: The caves are dangerous. Tons of ice from the ceilings may come crashing to the floor at any time. Tumbling avalanches are a constant threat through winter and early spring. Skiers and snowshoers are cautioned not to venture too close to the snowfield. The caves are exceptionally dangerous to enter or climb.

BOARDMAN LAKE AND LAKE EVAN TRAIL 704

**LENGTH: 0.8 mile   BEST SEASONS: summer, fall
LOW ELEVATION: 2800 ft.   HIGH: 3100 ft.   GAIN: 300 ft.**

TRAILHEAD ACCESS: From the Verlot Public Service Center, travel east on the Mtn. Loop Highway for 4.5 miles. Turn right (south) on the Schweitzer Creek Road 4020. Continue for 5 miles to the trailhead on the left.

PARKING AND FACILITIES: No toilet facilities at trailhead.

DESCRIPTION: For those wanting a picnic stop near the road, 12.8-acre Lake Evan provides a peaceful wooded setting. Most of the lakeshore is too marshy for use, but just off the trail is firm ground. After 100 yards the trail enters dense old-growth forest for 0.8 mile to the outlet of Boardman Lake. On the east shore of the lake is a campground with 5 campsites and a backcountry toilet. Please stay on the trail. There are rare plants located in this lake basin.

CHOCKWICH MTN. BIKE TRAIL 647.2

LENGTH: 2.5 miles BEST SEASONS: summer, fall
LOW ELEVATION: 1900 ft. HIGH: 28000 ft. GAIN: 900 ft.

GOAT LAKE SIDE TRAILHEAD ACCESS 1: From the Verlot Public Service Center, travel east on the Mtn. Loop Highway 22.8 miles to the Elliot Creek Road 4080. Turn right and continue 0.8 miles to the trailhead.

GOAT LAKE SIDE TRAILHEAD ACCESS 2: From Darrington Ranger Station, travel south along the Mtn. Loop Highway 20 for 22 miles to Elliot Creek Road 4080. Turn left and continue 0.8 miles to the trailhead.

PARKING AND FACILITIES: Parking available at the trailhead. This is a busy trailhead with limited parking. Please don't park in the turnaround area.

DESCRIPTION: Follow the Upper Elliot Creek Trail straight ahead from the trailhead. Continue 1 mile and turn left at the junction to follow the Chockwich Trail.

BEDAL SIDE TRAILHEAD ACCESS 1: From Verlot Public Service Center, travel east on the Mtn. Loop Highway 26 miles to Road 4096. Turn right and continue 2 miles to the trailhead.

BEDAL SIDE TRAILHEAD ACCESS 2: From Darrington Ranger Station, travel south along the Mtn. Loop Highway 20 for 21 miles to Road 4096. Turn left and continue 2 miles to the trailhead.

PARKING AND FACILITIES: Parking available at the trailhead. Parking is limited, so you might want to turn your vehicle around before leaving. Please don't park in the turnaround area.

DESCRIPTION: The trail continues on the old road, crossing Bedal Creek at 1/4 mile where there is a camp site. The ford can be difficult, especially early in the season. The ford at Chockwich creek can also be difficult in very high runoff conditions. Continue generally trending downward through big timber, then small alder groves and then openings with views of the upper Sauk valley until reaching the junction with Upper Elliot Creek Trail (647) at 2200 feet. Please note that bicycles are allowed only on Upper Elliot Creek Trail. Lower Elliot Creek trail is not a bike trail and the Goat Lake Trail enters Henry M. Jackson Wilderness where only foot traffic is permitted.

LENGTH: 0.1 mile   **BEST SEASONS:** spring, summer, winter, fall
LOW ELEVATION: 3600 ft.   **HIGH:** 3600 ft.   **GAIN:** 0 ft.

TRAILHEAD ACCESS: From the Verlot Public Service Center, travel east on the Mtn. Loop Highway for 15 miles. Turn left (north) on the Coal Lake Road 4060 and continue 4.4 miles to the trailhead.

PARKING AND FACILITIES: There is a parking lot and toilet at the trailhead.

DESCRIPTION: This pretty 6-acre lake is in a subalpine setting. Since it is a short hike to the lake, it is quite popular. It's an easy portage for canoes and rubber rafts, but there are a limited number of campsites around the lake. Expect crowds on summer weekends.

FORKS OF CANYON CREEK TRAIL 633

LENGTH: 1 mile   **BEST SEASONS:** spring, summer, fall
LOW ELEVATION: 1400 ft.   **HIGH:** 2400 ft.   **GAIN:** 1000 ft.

TRAILHEAD ACCESS: From the Verlot Public Service Center, travel west on the Mtn. Loop Highway 3.9 miles. Turn right (north) on Tupso Pass Road 41 and continue for 12.5 miles to Road 4140. Road 4140 is not maintained, be prepared for a brushy road. Go left down the road almost to end. Parking is best prior to the road's end in wide turnoff 0.25 mile before the trail start. The trail is not signed.

PARKING AND FACILITIES: Narrow trailhead with limited parking.

DESCRIPTION: This rough and infrequently maintained trail switchbacks downhill through beautiful old-growth timber. Beetle kill impacted a portion of this stand of timber. What was once old-growth is now standing snags and brush. A secluded campsite is found at the confluence of the forks of Canyon Creek. This spot is seldom visited and, because of its low elevation, is free of snow and accessible in late spring. This trail receives sporadic maintenance and can be very brushy.

FROG LAKE TRAIL 659

LENGTH: 1 mile   **BEST SEASONS:** spring, summer, fall, winter
LOW ELEVATION: 600 ft.   **HIGH:** 1000 ft.   **GAIN:** 400 ft.

TRAILHEAD ACCESS: At the four-way stop at Highway 530 and Mtn. Loop Highway, turn right and follow the road for 3.6 miles.

PARKING AND FACILITIES: Parking is on the right, just before the bridge.

DESCRIPTION: This trail provides a short nature hike, climbing steadily up the side of the hill, with views of Clear Creek far below. The trail emerges onto theroad after 0.8 mile, but makes a sharp turn back toward the lake. It passes through dense forest, eventually ending at 1.5-acre Frog Lake.

HAROLD ENGLES MEMORIAL GROVE TRAIL 642

LENGTH: 0.5 mile **BEST SEASONS:** summer, fall
LOW ELEVATION: 1750 ft. **HIGH:** 1800 ft. **GAIN:** 50 ft.

> **TRAILHEAD ACCESS:** From Darrington Ranger Station travel south along the Mtn. Loop Highway 20 for 16.3 miles to Sloan Creek Road 49. Turn left (east) and continue for 3.4 miles to the signboard and trailhead on right.
>
> **PARKING AND FACILITIES:** The road widens at the trailhead, there is limited parking.
>
> **DESCRIPTION:** The trail makes a gently winding loop along the flats of the North Fork Sauk River among dramatic forest with giant cedar trees, including a dense grove with interwoven boughs. Named in honor of a legendary early Darrington District Ranger, Harold Engles was a gentle giant of a man who hiked and climbed into his eighties. He is best known for an early ascent of 6870 ft. Three Fingers with Harry Bedal in their search for an appropriate lookout site. An interpretive plaque honoring him can be found on a cedar tree measuring 14 ft. in diameter. For river views head left through big trees, or turn right at the junction to find the dense cedar grove.

HEATHER LAKE TRAIL 701

LENGTH: 1.9 miles **BEST SEASONS:** spring, summer, fall
LOW ELEVATION: 1600 ft. **HIGH:** 2450 ft. **GAIN:** 850 ft.

> **TRAILHEAD ACCESS:** From the Verlot Public Service Center, travel east on the Mtn. Loop Highway 1 mile. Turn right (south) on the Pilchuck Road 42 and continue 1.5 miles to the trailhead on your left.
>
> **PARKING AND FACILITIES:** There is a parking lot and toilet facilities at the trailhead and a backcountry toilet at the lake.
>
> **DESCRIPTION:** Proceed through an old clear-cut as you climb gently up to a flat where the glacier-carved lake lies beneath the cliffs of Mt. Pilchuck. The lake is in a subalpine forest and meadow setting and is quite popular all months of the year. This lake can be quite crowded on summer weekends. Certain areas on the south side of the lake have a rocky shore and feature boulders, which offer the best opportunity for fishing access, wildflowers, and berry picking. A 0.7-mile trail has been built around the lake. Limited camping is available: please use existing sites. If choosing to have a campfire please use an existing fire ring and keep the fire small.
>
> Very limited camping is available; please use only existing sites. If choosing to have a campfire, please use an existing fire ring as burning sterilizes the soil and creates denuded areas. Remember to pack out everything you packed in.

LENGTH: 0.7 mile   BEST SEASONS: summer, fall
LOW ELEVATION: 3600 ft.   HIGH: 3700 ft.   GAIN: 100 ft.

TRAILHEAD ACCESS: From the Verlot Public Service Center, travel east on the Mtn. Loop Highway 15 miles. Turn left (north) onto Coal Lake Road 4060 and continue 4.8 miles to the trailhead at the end of the road.

PARKING AND FACILITIES: There is a parking lot at the trailhead. The north end area of the lake offers a backcountry toilet.

DESCRIPTION: The trail passes through a clear-cut unit (harvested in 1961) and then enters into old-growth timber, as it drops and rises to the lake.

The lake is surrounded by forest and is heavily fished. There is camping at the north and south ends of the lake. Access to the trail, which continues on to North Lake, is at the northeast end of the lake where it begins to switch-back up the hillside.

LAKE TWENTY-TWO TRAIL 702

LENGTH: 2.7 miles   BEST SEASONS: spring, summer, fall
LOW ELEVATION: 1000 ft.   HIGH: 2500 ft.   GAIN: 1500 ft.

TRAILHEAD ACCESS: From the Verlot Public Service Center, travel east on the Mtn. Loop Highway 2 miles to the trailhead on the right.

PARKING AND FACILITIES: There is a parking lot and toilet facilities at the trailhead.

DESCRIPTION: The trail follows Twenty-Two Creek, climbing continuously, but not steeply, through old-growth timber and a large talus slope. The trail is used year-round, and is very crowded on summer weekends.

This is one of three Research Natural Areas on the district. It was set aside in 1947 to study the effects on water, wildlife, and timber of an area left in its virgin state, as compared to similar areas under intensive management. Thus, in order to help protect the characteristics of the area, OVERNIGHT CAMPING AND CAMPFIRES ARE NOT PERMITTED.

The lake is in a glacier-carved basin on the north flank of Mt. Pilchuck. Fishing can sometimes be quite good as the lake is 53 ft. deep. A one-mile loop trail around the lake passes through meadows and rock slides; be on the lookout for wildlife. Please remain on the trail to prevent erosion and reduce impact on rare plants.

LOOKOUT TREE TRAIL 783.1

LENGTH: 1 mile **BEST SEASONS:** spring, summer, fall
LOW ELEVATION: 1000 ft.   **HIGH:** 1200 ft.   **GAIN:** 200 ft.

TRAILHEAD ACCESS: To access the trailhead, follow the Mtn. Loop Highway for 10 miles to the end of the pavement and continue on gravel for 2.3 miles to a small pullout on the right. The trailhead is just prior to reaching Lyle Creek.

PARKING AND FACILITIES: There is a small pull-out parking area on the right. No toilet facilites.

DESCRIPTION: This trail descends to the Sauk River, passing through beautiful groves of ancient cedar. At the bottom of the first hill look to the right for the remains of a huge, 48 ft. circumference cedar tree.The tree once served as a fire lookout for the ranger stationed at the former nearby Sauk Ranger Station. Though the tree has largely collapsed, some spikes that were used as footholds to ascend to the lookout point can still be seen. The cedar is a testament to the ancient forests that railroaders harvested from 1920 to 1940. The trail continues to descend until it meets the Sauk Lumber Company's old railroad grade. Remains of the decaying train trestles, now covered with moss, can be seen. The trail comes to an abrupt end where it was washed out in 1995.

MALLARDY RIDGE (WALT BAILEY'S) TRAIL 706

LENGTH: 3.5 miles **BEST SEASONS:** summer, fall
LOW ELEVATION: 3000 ft.   **HIGH:** 4200 ft.   **GAIN:** 1200 ft.

TRAILHEAD ACCESS: From the Verlot Public Service Center, drive east on the Mtn. Loop Highway 7 miles to the Mallardy Road 4030. Turn right and follow this road for 1.4 miles to the junction with Road 4032. Turn right and follow this road for 7.1 miles.

PARKING AND FACILITIES: Parking is limited, so you might want to turn your vehicle around before leaving to hike.

DESCRIPTION: Also known as the Walt Bailey Trail, much of this trail was constructed by Walt Bailey, a former Civilian Conservation Corps (CCC) employee, who recruited and organized the efforts of many dedicated volunteers. Within a mile of the trailhead, the trail enters the Morning Star Natural Resources Conservation Area (NRCA). This NRCA is managed by the Washington State Department of Natural Resources primarily to protect high-quality wetlands, fragile subalpine meadows, sensitive plant communities, and habitat for threatened, endangered, and rare wildlife species. Opportunities for low-impact public use are allowed if they do not adversely affect ecological processes, and are provided with this trail leading to a primitive backcountry camp in the vicinity of the Cutthroat Lakes. The trail passes through an old-growth forest of hemlock and Pacific silver-fir, skirting fragile wetlands and traversing talus slopes in the transition from forest to a subalpine mountain heather vegetation zone at the Cutthroat Lakes. The plant communities of the subalpine zone are extremely sensitive to trampling damage. Please stay on trails, rock, or snow to avoid trampling. This is a NO CAMPFIRE zone to protect the fragile subalpine parkland vegetation. Campers should bring a stove. There are no toilets. Please use "Leave No Trace" methods.

From here, the trail continues on to the Bald Mountain Trail and Ashland Lakes. Hiking the Walt Bailey Trail will reward you with spectacular scenery and an appreciation for the dedication of Walt and the numerous volunteers who built this trail. For more information about the NRCA, contact the DNR at 360-856-3500.

MT. DICKERMAN TRAIL 710

LENGTH: 4.3 miles   BEST SEASONS: summer, fall
LOW ELEVATION: 2000 ft.   HIGH: 5723 ft.   GAIN: 3723 ft.

TRAILHEAD ACCESS: From the Verlot Public Service Center, travel east along the Mtn. Loop Highway, 16.6 miles to the trailhead on the left (north) side of the highway.

PARKING AND FACILITIES: There is a parking lot and toilet facilities at trailhead.

DESCRIPTION: This trail switchbacks steeply for 3 miles through a dark forest of timber that was replanted in 1915 after a major forest fire. The transition area from the timber presents some exposed crossings that are extremely hazardous when holding snow or ice. Then the trail rises above the timberline to an alpine meadow with masses of wildflowers in July and August.

The trail is generally in good condition and there are views in all directions as the trail climbs to the 5723 ft. summit. The views to the south of Big Four Mountain and Del Campo Peak are especially good. The meadows and summit remain snow-covered until midsummer. No water can be found on this hike.

MT. FORGOTTEN MEADOWS (PERRY CREEK) TRAIL 711

LENGTH: 4.8 miles   BEST SEASONS: summer, fall
LOW ELEVATION: 2000 ft.   HIGH: 5000 ft.   GAIN: 3000 ft.

TRAILHEAD ACCESS: From the Verlot Public Service Center, travel east on the Mtn. Loop Highway 16.6 miles to the trailhead on the left (north) side of the highway. The trailhead is located at the west side of the parking lot, opposite Mt. Dickerman trailhead.

PARKING AND FACILITIES: There is a parking lot and toilet at the trailhead.

DESCRIPTION: For 1 mile the trail contours through big cedar and Douglas fir trees with occasional glimpses of Big Four rising dramatically across the South Fork Stillaguamish River valley. The trail then continues on the old roadway for 0.25 miles to the old trailhead, entering a stand of second growth hemlock. Once you break out of the trees, the trail is rocky but well defined. It climbs continuously, but not steeply, through timber and open talus slopes that contain an outstanding assortment of ferns in a rich botanical area. Views of the many waterfalls across the valley are spectacular. The falls, reached at 2.9 miles, provide a picnic and resting spot. From here the trail passes through old-growth forest for another 1.7 miles until the first meadow is reached. The trail continues through the meadows, which provide experienced mountain climbers access to 6005 ft. Mt. Forgotten. The views from the meadows are spectacular— north to Mt. Baker, east to Glacier Peak, and south to Mt. Rainier.

Perry Creek was recently established as a research natural area because of its unique plant communities. For this reason overnight camping and campfires are not recommended. Hikers are asked to remain on established trails.

MT. HIGGINS TRAIL 640

LENGTH: 4.5 miles   BEST SEASONS: summer, fall
LOW ELEVATION: 1600 ft.   HIGH: 4800 ft.   GAIN: 3200 ft.

> **TRAILHEAD ACCESS:** From the Darrington Ranger Station, take Highway 530 west for 11.8 miles. Just past milepost 38, take the road to the right (north), signed C-Post Road. Continue on the road for 2.8 miles after crossing over the North Fork Stillaguamish River. The road dead-ends at the trailhead. The trail is on the right (east side) of the road.
>
> **PARKING AND FACILITIES:** Limited parking.
>
> **DESCRIPTION:** The first mile of the trail passes through a clear-cut. This portion of the trail is administered by the Washington State Department of Natural Resources. At a junction at approximately 3.3 miles, the trail to the left (west) drops down to 7.6-acre Myrtle Lake. At an elevation of 3700 ft. a marshy shore surrounds this quiet lake. The main trail going right (east) climbs slightly, passing through swampy meadows for 0.2 mile. Then the trail starts a gradual climb passing through boulder fields and dense forest until reaching the summit. This is the site of the former Mt. Higgins Lookouts, which was used for fire detection in the summers from 1926 to 1949. The views of the surrounding mountains are outstanding—Glacier Peak to the east; White Horse, Three Fingers, and Mt. Rainier to the south. Looking west offers views of the Olympics and Puget Sound.

MOUNT PILCHUCK LOOKOUT TRAIL 700

LENGTH: 3 miles   BEST SEASONS: summer, fall
LOW ELEVATION: 3100 ft.   HIGH: 5324 ft.   GAIN: 2224 ft.

> **TRAILHEAD ACCESS:** From the Verlot Public Service Center, travel east on the Mtn. Loop Highway 1 mile. Turn right (south) on the Pilchuck Road 42 and continue for 6.9 miles to the trailhead.

PARKING AND FACILITIES: There is a parking lot, toilet, and limited primitive camping at the trailhead.

DESCRIPTION: The trail travels through old-growth forest and follows the edge of an area clear-cut by the Washington State Department of Natural Resources in 1977. When trail is partially snow covered, often well into June, route finding is difficult. At approximately one mile the trail enters Washington State Park land. The final approach to the summit is a steep boulder scramble that can be particularly difficult in wet or icy conditions. The 5324 ft. summit has views of the Cascades, Olympics, and Puget Sound.

There is a Forest Service lookout on top maintained by the Everett Mountaineers and managed by Washington State Parks. The Forest Service maintains the trail under an agreement with Washington State Parks. Washington State Parks administered a ski area here from 1957 to 1980. The former ski slope looks like a shortcut, but it is brushy, steep, and hard going. The trail is often muddy and drinking water is scarce.Mt. Pilchuck was likely among the long ridge of snowy mountains sighted by the English explorer George Vancouver during the spring of 1792. This peak stands well in front of the main Cascade Range, and is rather conspicuous when viewed from Puget Sound. The trail is usually snow-covered until midsummer, and is very popular on a clear day.

NORTH FORK SAUK FALLS 660

LENGTH: 0.2 mile   BEST SEASONS: spring, summer, fall
LOW ELEVATION: 1400 ft.   HIGH: 1500 ft.   GAIN: 100 ft.

TRAILHEAD ACCESS:

Access 1: From the Darrington Ranger Station, take Mtn. Loop Highway 20 along the west side of the Sauk River. Drive 19.7 miles to Sloan Creek Road 49 and turn left. Follow this road for 1 mile to the trailhead on the right.

Access 2: From the Verlot Public Service Center, drive east along the Mtn. Loop Highway 27 miles to Sloan Creek Road 49 and turn right. Drive this road for 1 mile to the trailhead on the right.

PARKING AND FACILITIES: There is a parking lot at the trailhead.

DESCRIPTION: This short trail descends 200 ft. to the base of a large waterfall. It is worth the half-hour diversion for anyone traveling along the Mtn. Loop since the 45 ft. high falls are spectacular.

NORTH LAKE TRAIL 712

LENGTH: 2.5 miles   BEST SEASONS: summer, fall
LOW ELEVATION: 3600 ft.   HIGH: 4100 ft.   GAIN: 500 ft.

TRAILHEAD ACCESS: From the Verlot Public Service Center, travel east on Mtn. Loop Highway for 15 miles. Turn left (north) on the Coal Lake Road 4060 and continue for 4.8 miles to the Independence Lake trailhead.

PARKING AND FACILITIES: No backcountry toilet is available at North Lake.

DESCRIPTION: The trail to North Lake begins off the trail to Independence Lake. At the northeast end of Independence Lake, the trail goes up the hillside in a steep climb, switchbacking for 1 mile until it reaches a ridge. This vantage point provides views of Three Fingers Mountain and Mt. Baker to the north. The trail continues east for 0.5 mile and reaches a second ridge with a view of Glacier Peak, other prominent peaks, and North Lake lying in a basin 700 ft. below. At this point, one can either enjoy the view and turn back, or descend to the lake where there are limited campsites.

This trail does not become snow-free until midsummer.

OLD GOVERNMENT TRAIL 733

LENGTH: 1.7 miles   **BEST SEASONS:** summer, fall
LOW ELEVATION: 2100 ft.   **HIGH:** 2400 ft.   **GAIN:** 300 ft.

TRAILHEAD ACCESS: From the Verlot Public Service Center, travel east on the Mtn. Loop Highway 19.4 miles to the trailhead on the left at Barlow Pass.

PARKING AND FACILITIES: There is a parking lot and toilet facilities at the Barlow Pass trailhead.

DESCRIPTION: This trail begins off of Barlow Point Trail 709 after 0.3 mile and proceeds north and west as it gently descends the South Fork Stillaguamish River valley. This route follows parts of the old Everett and Monte Cristo Railway grade and an old trail that paralleled the railroad. This is a pleasant, short, lowland forest walk.

OLD SAUK TRAIL 728

LENGTH: 3 miles   **BEST SEASONS:** spring, summer, fall, winter
LOW ELEVATION: 600 ft.   **HIGH:** 600 ft.   **GAIN:** 0 ft.

TRAILHEAD ACCESS: From the Darrington Ranger Station, take Mtn. Loop Highway 20 along the west side of the Sauk River. Follow this road for 4 miles, going past the Clear Creek Campground. The trailhead is on the left.

PARKING AND FACILITIES: There is a parking lot at the trailhead.

DESCRIPTION: This trail winds in and out of the forest, following the Sauk River. The old cedar stumps, surrounded by mossy vegetation, are remnants of what once was an old-growth forest. The serenity of the river and the frequent presence of wildlife and waterfowl make this a pleasant hike. During the summer and fall, salmon and steelhead are sometimes seen as they go up the river to spawn.

LENGTH: 2.2 miles   BEST SEASONS: summer, fall
LOW ELEVATION: 3200 ft.   HIGH: 4000 ft.   GAIN: 800 ft.

TRAILHEAD ACCESS: From the Darrington Ranger Station, take the Mtn. Loop Highway 20 along the west side of the Sauk River for 9.2 miles to Road 2080. Turn right (west) and follow this road for 1.1 miles. Stay right at the junction and continue on Road 2081. Continue 1.7 miles and stay right at the junction. Continue 0.3 miles and stay right at the junction. Continue 2.3 miles to the trailhead parking area.

PARKING AND FACILITIES: Limited parking at trailhead.

DESCRIPTION: This trail begins at the end of Road 2086 and follows an abandoned logging road about 1/3 mile until it enters old-growth forest and narrows to a trail.The trail climbs gradually up the hill, crossing several small creeks winding in and out of trees. Once on the ridge, the trail gets easier and soon drops down to the lake, surrounded by trees, boulders, and marshy terrain. Campsites are located on the northeast side among the trees.

PINNACLE LAKE TRAIL 703

LENGTH: 1.8 miles   BEST SEASONS: summer, fall,
LOW ELEVATION: 2700 ft.   HIGH: 3800 ft.   GAIN: 1100 ft.

TRAILHEAD ACCESS: From the Verlot Public Service Center, travel east on Mtn. Loop Highway 4.5 miles. Turn right (south) on the Schweitzer Creek Road 4020. Continue 2.3 miles to the Bear Lake Road 4021 and continue for 3.4 miles to the trailhead.

PARKING AND FACILITIES: There is a parking lot at the trailhead.

DESCRIPTION: Follow Bear Lake Trail 661 for 0.2 mile and then take the left fork. The trail is rocky, rough, and muddy sometimes. It crosses Bear Creek and then switchbacks through timber, breaking into alpine terrain after 1.5 miles. The lake, sitting in rocky terrain at the base of a steep shore, has several camping areas above it and to the north.

SUNRISE MINE TRAIL 707

LENGTH: 3 miles   BEST SEASONS: summer, fall
LOW ELEVATION: 2200 ft.   HIGH: 4600 ft.   GAIN: 2400 ft.

TRAILHEAD ACCESS: From the Verlot Public Service Center, travel east on Mtn. Loop Highway 17.1 miles. Turn right (south) on the Sunrise Mine Road 4065 and continue 2.2 miles to the trailhead at the end.

PARKING AND FACILITIES: Parking is limited, you may want to turn your vehicle around before leaving to hike. Please don't park in the turnaround area.

DESCRIPTION: The trail begins in an area clear-cut in 1967 and quickly enters the timber. At 0.5 mile the trail makes a slippery log crossing of the South Fork Stillaguamish River and then climbs steeply to the ridge between Morning Star and Sperry peaks.

The trail, which is rough in places, is one of the most rugged and beautiful areas on the district and also one of the least visited. It is used in large part by mountain climbers as access for climbing Morning Star, Sperry, Vesper, and Del Campo peaks. The trail is covered with snow until midsummer. Excellent views of the surrounding basin and valley are available the entire length of the trail.

Rock cairns mark the trail in the upper basin. Hikers should use caution just below Headlee Pass. This steep, narrow, rocky chute is notorious for falling rocks. In the vicinity of Headlee Pass, the trail enters the Morning Star Natural Resources Conservation Area (NRCA). There are no designated campsites and no toilet facilities in this area of the NRCA. This is a NO CAMPFIRE zone to protect the fragile subalpine an alpine vegetation. Hikers should carry a stove and use "Leave No Trace" methods of backcountry travel.

WEDEN CREEK (GOTHIC BASIN) TRAIL 724

LENGTH: 3.3 miles   BEST SEASONS: summer, fall
LOW ELEVATION: 2300 ft.   HIGH: 5000 ft.   GAIN: 2700 ft.

TRAILHEAD ACCESS: From the Verlot Public Service Center, travel east on the Mtn. Loop Highway 19.5 miles; park at Barlow Pass and proceed on foot for 1 mile on the Monte Cristo Road. The trailhead is on the right (just before the Sauk River crossing).

PARKING AND FACILITIES: There is a parking lot and toilet facilities at Barlow Pass.

DESCRIPTION: This old miner's trail climbs steeply through timber then begins a long traverse across steep terrain, where forest vegetation gives way to subalpine mountain heather. Before entering Gothic Basin, the trail enters the Morning Star Natural Resources Conservation Area (NRCA). This NRCA is managed by the Washington State Department of Natural Resources primarily to protect high-quality wetlands, fragile subalpine meadows, sensitive plant communities, and habitat for threatened, endangered, and rare wildlife species. Opportunities for low-impact public use are allowed if they do not adversely affect ecological processes. The plant communities in the subalpine and alpine zones are extremely sensitive to trampling damage. Please stay on trails, rock, or snow to avoid trampling this fragile vegetation.

Even though this is one of the most spectacularly beautiful areas on the district, the trail is recommended only for experienced hikers with ice axes, as three potentially dangerous snow gullies are crossed en route. The basin can sometimes remain snow-covered into early September. The trail ends at Foggy Lake where mountaineers gain access to climb Del Campo and Gothic peaks. Foggy Lake, which is 35 ft. deep, is barren of fish and is usually frozen all year long. This is a NO CAMPFIRE zone to protect the fragile subalpine vegetation. Hikers should bring a stove and use "Leave No Trace" techniques for backcountry travel.

For more information about the NRCA, contact the DNR at 360-856-3500.

WHITE CHUCK BENCH TRAIL 731

**LENGTH: 7 miles   BEST SEASONS: spring, summer, fall
LOW ELEVATION: 1000 ft.   HIGH: 1600 ft.   GAIN: 600 ft.**

TRAILHEAD ACCESS: From the Darrington Ranger Station, take the Mtn. Loop Highway 20 along the west side of the Sauk River for 10 miles. Go left over the bridge on Road 22, which is paved to the White Chuck boat launch. Continue 0.75 miles to the small trailhead parking on the left.

PARKING AND FACILITIES: Parking is limited. Please use the toilets at the White Chuck boat launch as there are none at the trailhead.

DESCRIPTION: With modest ups and downs, this trail is a pleasant hike along the west side of the Sauk River. The cedar stumps, surrounded by mossy vegetation and an assortment of ferns, make this trail a hiker's delight.

Past a young hemlock stand, the west end of the trail rewards hikers with a spectacular view of the river below and the towering Pugh Mountain. Weaving among trees, the trail skirts the ridge before descending to cross Black Oak Creek at 1 mile. The trail continues through alder and second growth, as it winds along the White Chuck River. About 1 mile from Black Oak the trail was damaged in the floods of 2003 and 2006. One can follow the old trail but be forewarned that it will be brushy and large segments have been consumed by the river. There are plans to rebuild the trail in the future.

YOUTH-ON-AGE TRAIL 738

**LENGTH: 0.3 miles   BEST SEASONS: summer, fall
LOW ELEVATION: 1400 ft.   HIGH: 1400 ft.   GAIN: 0 ft.**

TRAILHEAD ACCESS: From Verlot Public Service Center, travel east on the Mtn. Loop 7.25 miles to the trailhead on the right.

PARKING AND FACILITIES: There is a parking lot and toilet at the trailhead.

DESCRIPTION: This mostly-paved interpretive trail circles through mossy old growth forest, giant Sitka spruce, hemlock, devil's club, and ferns along the banks of the South Fork Stillaguamish River. To learn more about the features indicated by the numbered signs, pick up an interpretive guide from the Verlot Public Service Center. A short, peaceful walk in the woods, Youth-On-Age is a gentle introduction to the ecology of the area, named for the piggy-backed leaves of a species of saxifrage plant found along the trail.

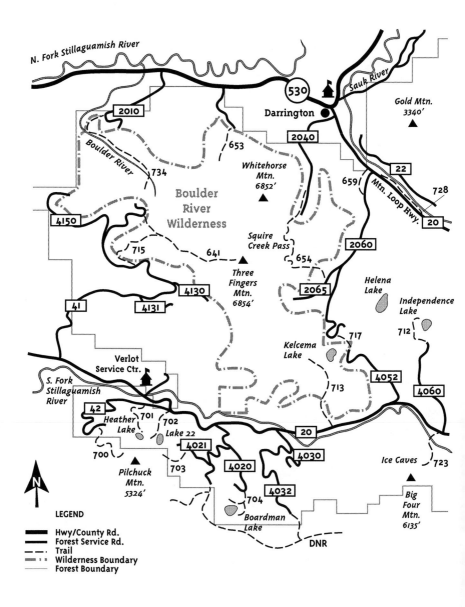

N. Fork Stillaguamish River

Sauk River

530

Darrington

Gold Mtn.
3340'

2010

2040

Boulder River

734

653

Whitehorse
Mtn.
6852'

22

728

20

659

Mtn. Loop Hwy.

Boulder
River
Wilderness

4150

715

641

Squire
Creek Pass

654

2060

Helena
Lake

Independence
Lake

712

Three
Fingers
Mtn.
6854'

2065

41

4130

4131

717

Kelcema
Lake

713

4052

4060

Verlot
Service Ctr.

S. Fork
Stillaguamish
River

42

701

702

Heather
Lake

Lake 22

20

4021

700

703

4020

4030

Ice Caves

723

Pilchuck
Mtn.
5324'

4032

Big
Four
Mtn.
6135'

704

Boardman
Lake

DNR

N

LEGEND

━━━ Hwy/County Rd.
━━━ Forest Service Rd.
─ ─ · Trail
▨ ▨ ▨ Wilderness Boundary
─────── Forest Boundary

*Maps in this trail guide are for general orientation only and are not to scale. Please use a
USDA Forest Service or other detailed topographic map for accurate and specific information.*

BOULDER RIVER WILDERNESS

The Boulder River Wilderness contains 49,000 acres of land, 25 miles of trails, and has an elevation range from 1200 ft. to 7000 ft. There are nine small lakes and the terrain is fairly rugged, with moderate to steep slopes. Boulder River, a tributary to the North Fork Stillaguamish, runs approximately ten miles through the northwest section of the wilderness. Large, old-growth timber is found in the lower reaches of the Boulder River drainage.

Present recreation use is heavy in some areas and consists primarily of hiking, fishing, and hunting. To help protect wilderness resources and provide you and others with quality wilderness experiences, please familiarize yourself with Leave No Trace, Wilderness Regulations, and other information provided in the Introduction to this guide.

BOULDER RIVER TRAIL 734

LENGTH: 4 miles   **BEST SEASONS:** spring, summer, winter, fall
LOW ELEVATION: 1000 ft.   **HIGH:** 1400 ft.   **GAIN:** 400 ft.

TRAILHEAD ACCESS: From the Darrington Ranger Station, take Highway 530 west for 8.2 miles to the French Creek turnoff (milepost 41) and turn left (south) onto Road 2010. Continue 3.7 miles to the trailhead parking lot.

PARKING AND FACILITIES: There is a parking lot at the trailhead and a toilet along the road at 1 mile from Highway 530, across from dispersed campsites.

DESCRIPTION: This trail is a pleasant hike along Boulder River. The trail enters a dense stand of virgin timber and crosses a number of small creeks. At 0.9 mile, a way trail drops down to where you can find the remnants of an old shelter and several nice camping spots.

At 1.2 miles there are a series of cascades and waterfalls seen across Boulder River on the opposite bank. A way trail leads to the base of the falls.

At about 2.5 miles the timber is thick and the river is seldom seen. At 4 miles the trail descends to end at Boulder River where there are several campsites. Please be prepared deal with your waste properly: it is difficult to cat hole 200 feet from camps, trail and water due to brush and steep terrain; and remember to pack out all that you packed in. At one time the trail continued on to the lookout on Three Fingers. Crossing Boulder River is difficult.

The use of livestock is prohibited on this trail.

DEER CREEK PASS TRAIL 717

LENGTH: 0.5 miles **BEST SEASONS:** summer, fall,
LOW ELEVATION: 3100 ft. **HIGH:** 3400 ft. **GAIN:** 300 ft.

TRAILHEAD ACCESS: From Verlot Public Service Center, travel east on the Mtn. Loop Highway 12.5 miles to Deer Creek Road 4052 on the left (north). Follow this road 4.2 miles to the Kelcema Lake trailhead on the left. Walk 100 feet further up the road and watch for the trail on the left.

PARKING AND FACILITIES: There is a backcountry toilet at Lake Kelcema only.

DESCRIPTION: This trail is rarely maintained, but it offers rapid elevation gain to peek-a-boo views of Three Fingers, Mt. Bullon, Jumbo, and others. In the late summer and early fall, look for ripe huckleberries.

EIGHT-MILE TRAIL 654.1

LENGTH: 2.5 miles **BEST SEASONS:** summer, fall,
LOW ELEVATION: 1600 ft. **HIGH:** 4000 ft. **GAIN:** 2400 ft.

TRAILHEAD ACCESS: From the Darrington Ranger Station, take Mtn. Loop Highway 20 along the west side of the Sauk River. Follow this road for approximately 3.3 miles. At the intersection with Clear Creek Campground and Road 20, turn right (west) on Road 2060. Follow this road for 8 miles to the trailhead on the right.

PARKING AND FACILITIES: Narrow trailhead with limited parking.

DESCRIPTION: This trail begins with a gentle climb, following an abandoned road. The trail is popular with rock climbers because it passes Three-O'clock Rock on the south side of Jumbo Mountain. From there the trail climbs steeply up the mountain over a long series of switchbacks, eventually meeting Squire Creek Trail at Squire Creek Pass.

Cascading waterfalls along the way make this an enjoyable hike. Mountain goats frequent the area. During late summer ripe huckleberries grow at the pass. A loop trip (which requires a second car) can be made by taking the Squire Creek Trail 654, which leads to the Squire Creek Road 2040. (See Squire Creek Trail 654 for further information.)

GOAT FLAT-SADDLE LAKE-THREE FINGERS 641

LENGTH: 6.7 miles **BEST SEASONS:** summer, fall
LOW ELEVATION: 3000 ft. **HIGH:** 6854 ft. **GAIN:** 3854 ft.

TRAILHEAD ACCESS: From the Verlot Public Service Center, travel west on the Mtn. Loop Highway for 3.9 miles. Turn right (north) on the Tupso Pass Road 41 and follow this road for 18 miles to the trailhead.

PARKING AND FACILITIES: There is a parking lot, there are no toilet facilities at the trailhead.

DESCRIPTION: A rough, root-filled trail travels from Tupso Pass through dense forest to 4-acre Saddle Lake at 2.5 miles. In the early 1970s a shelter was constructed by the Everett Mountaineers at the edge of the meadows near the lake. No camping is allowed within 200 ft. of Saddle Lake. Travel 2.3 miles farther through subalpine meadows and timber to Goat Flat. This area is often crowded on summer and fall weekends. Please protect the fragile vegetation by using only existing campsites. Fires are prohibited from Saddle Lake to Three Fingers.

The trail reaches Tin Pan Gap after 6.2 miles. It is a technical climb requiring climbing expertise and equipment from this point onward. Three Fingers glacier must be traversed, followed by a rocky scramble and ascent on steep ladders to the lookout on the south peak of Three Fingers Mountain. The lookout was built in 1933 and is listed on the National Register of Historic Places. It was necessary to blast off the top 10 to 15 feet of the peak in order to build the structure. Old telephone wires can still be seen intermittently along the Three Fingers Trail. In 1986, the Everett Mountaineers assumed maintenance of the lookout.

KELCEMA LAKE 718

LENGTH: 0.6 mile   BEST SEASONS: spring, summer, fall
LOW ELEVATION: 3100 ft.   HIGH: 3200 ft.   GAIN: 100 ft.

TRAILHEAD ACCESS: From the Verlot Public Service Center, follow Mtn. Loop Highway for 12.5 miles to Deer Creek Road 4052 on the left. Follow this road for 4.2 miles to the trailhead on the left.

PARKING AND FACILITIES: There is a small parking lot at the trailhead. A backcountry toilet is provided at Lake Kelcema.

DESCRIPTION: This is a short and pleasant, but often muddy hike for beginning backpackers or an afternoon outing. The trail provides access for fishermen and an easy portage for small boats and rubber rafts. The 23-acre lake sits in a subalpine setting, surrounded by trees and vegetation. Huckleberries grow here in late summer and early fall. Use only existing fire rings and burn only wood which is both dead and down.

MARTEN CREEK TRAIL 713

LENGTH: 3.3 miles   BEST SEASONS, summer, fall
LOW ELEVATION: 1400 ft.   HIGH: 2800 ft.   GAIN: 1400 ft.

TRAILHEAD ACCESS: From the Verlot Public Service Center, travel east on Mtn. Loop Highway 9.6 miles to the trailhead at Marten Creek. **PARKING AND FACILITIES:** Limited parking along the Mountain Loop Highway.

DESCRIPTION: This route once served the Marten Creek Mines and extended over Granite Pass to Darrington. The first mile of trail is an old mining road from the 1940s. It climbs steeply as it passes an experimental tree plantation established in 1915 after a major fire. These tree seedlings were taken from various locations and elevations to compare success of growth over the years. After the first mile, the trail levels out and emerges into a large brushy basin where there are great views of Three Fingers. At 2.5 miles it crosses Marten Creek and continues for 0.8 mile to the site of an old mine. At this point, the trail disappears in the brush and access to Granite Pass becomes a matter of cross-country travel. There is a good campsite located in the brush prior to the Marten Creek crossing. This trail provides good opportunities for solitude in a lowland forest.

NIEDERPRUM (WHITEHORSE) TRAIL 653

LENGTH: 2 miles   **BEST SEASONS:** spring, summer, fall
LOW ELEVATION: 800 ft.   **HIGH:** 3200 ft.   **GAIN:** 2400 ft.

> **TRAILHEAD ACCESS:** From the Darrington Ranger Station, take Highway 530 west for 6 miles to the Whitehorse store. Turn left (south) on the Mine Road and follow it for 0.75 mile to the bridge over Moose Creek, which is closed to vehicles.
>
> **PARKING AND FACILITIES:** Limited parking is available. The mine road, though short, is steep and rough. Park just before the bridge over Moose Creek and proceed on foot.
>
> **DESCRIPTION:** Cross the old road bridge and walk the road for 1.75 miles to reach the trailhead on the right. This old mining trail is used primarily by climbers seeking the summit of Whitehorse Mountain. Only the first 1.4 miles of the old trail is periodically maintained. Above this, the route rapidly degenerates into very steep and sometimes muddy way trails, then into thick brush until no evidence of a trail remains.

Only experienced mountaineers should venture beyond here. Even the maintained part of the trail is steep enough to tax the cardiovascular system of climbers and hardy hikers. The trail offers glimpses of the Stillaguamish Valley and views of Round Mountain and Segelson Ridge, with Mt. Baker dominating the northernmost views.

SQUIRE CREEK TRAIL 654

LENGTH: 5.7 miles   **BEST SEASONS:** summer, fall
LOW ELEVATION: 1600 ft.   **HIGH:** 4000 ft.   **GAIN:** 2400 ft.

> **TRAILHEAD ACCESS:** From the Darrington Ranger Station, take the Mtn. Loop Highway along the west side of the Sauk River. Follow this road for approximately 1.4 miles to Darrington Street. Turn right and follow this road for 3.75 miles to the end.

NOTE: The trail is maintained, but the first two miles of road are not maintained.

PARKING AND FACILITIES: There is a limited parking area at road end.

DESCRIPTION: In 2002, a massive slide came down from Jumbo Mountain and blocked the access road 2 miles from the trailhead. To reach the old trailhead, pass through returning alder and across a small feeder stream while marveling at the enormous amount of mountainside that came down and blocked Squire Creek below you. After a couple hundred yards, watch for a glimpse of the old road bed and climb up slope to attain the road again and walk the two miles to the old trailhead. The trail begins on an abandoned logging road and crosses numerous creeks and springs, passing through patches of old-growth timber. Some of the most spectacular views of Three Fingers, Mt. Bullon, and the seldom-seen cliffs of Whitehorse are visible from the trail as it climbs steadily upward.

At 3.5 miles the trail crosses a boulder field and reaches a small stream followed by a few switchbacks. There are huckleberry bushes along the trail. When reaching the pass there are views to the east. To see to the south you must climb on up to the ridge. There are numerous tarns in the pass, nestled here and there among the huckleberry bushes and heather. Mountain goats are known to frequent the area. There is limited camping here. Use existing camp sites and please bring a camp stove as down and dead wood is scarce.

For a loop trip (which requires a second car) you can continue down the other side of the pass towards Clear Creek on the Eight-mile Trail 654.1 ending on the Clear Creek Road 2065.

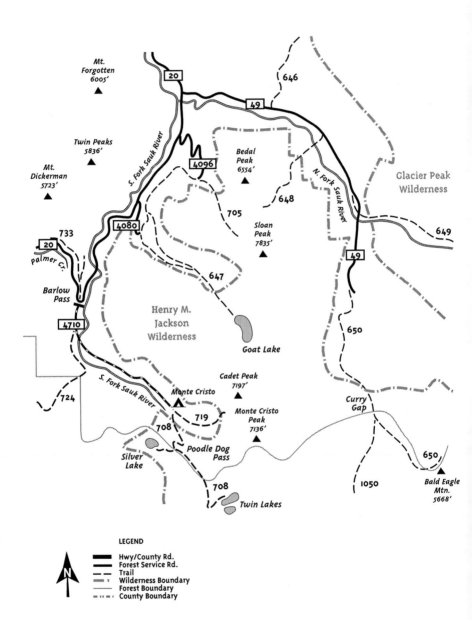

Mt. Forgotten 6005'

Twin Peaks 5836'

Mt. Dickerman 5723'

Bedal Peak 6554'

Glacier Peak Wilderness

S. Fork Sauk River

N. Fork Sauk River

646

49

4096

705

648

649

733

20

4080

Palmer Cr.

Barlow Pass

4710

Sloan Peak 7835'

647

49

650

Henry M. Jackson Wilderness

Goat Lake

S. Fork Sauk River

724

Monte Cristo

719

708

Cadet Peak 7197'

Monte Cristo Peak 7136'

Curry Gap

Silver Lake

Poodle Dog Pass

708

Twin Lakes

650

1050

Bald Eagle Mtn. 5668'

LEGEND

N	Hwy/County Rd.
	Forest Service Rd.
	Trail
	Wilderness Boundary
	Forest Boundary
	County Boundary

Maps in this trail guide are for general orientation only and are not to scale. Please use a USDA Forest Service or other detailed topographic map for accurate and specific information.

HENRY M. JACKSON WILDERNESS

The Henry M. Jackson Wilderness contains 103,591 acres (76,200 on the Mt. Baker-Snoqualmie National Forest), and 49 miles of trails with an elevation range from 2350 ft. to 8000 ft. The area is adjacent to the existing Glacier Peak Wilderness. Streams in the northern portion of this area drain into the Sauk River, while the Skykomish River drains the southern portion.

Game abounds in the wilderness; cougar, mountain goat, hoary marmot and blue grouse inhabit the area. Black tail deer is the major big game. The terrain is extremely rugged with narrow wooded valleys rising rapidly to open slopes and meadowlands that transition quickly to rock and ice. There are approximately 30 lakes, which receive moderate fishing pressure. The area is rich in mining history, particularly near the former town site of Monte Cristo, with many acres of patented mining claims within the wilderness.

The trails listed are within the Darrington Ranger District only and include about 35 miles of trails. To help protect wilderness resources and provide you and others with quality wilderness experiences, please familiarize yourself with Leave No Trace, Wilderness Regulations and other information provided in the Introduction to this guide.

BALD EAGLE (CURRY GAP) TRAIL 650

LENGTH: 9.5 miles   BEST SEASONS: summer, fall
LOW ELEVATION: 3300 ft.   HIGH: 5600 ft.   GAIN: 2300 ft.

TRAILHEAD ACCESS

Access 1: From the Verlot Public Service Center, drive east along the Mtn. Loop Highway 27 miles and turn right onto Sloan Creek Road 49. Follow it for 9.5 miles passing Sloan Creek Campground at 6.5 miles, to the trailhead .5 mile past the stock unloading ramp and toilet.

Access 2: From the Darrington Ranger Station, take the Mtn. Loop Highway 20 along the west side of the Sauk River. Drive 16.3 miles to the Sloan Creek Road 49 and turn left. Follow above directions from here.

PARKING AND FACILITIES: Stock vehicle parking and unloading ramp. Stock campground. Toilet facilities.

DESCRIPTION: This trail provides access to the Glacier Peak Wilderness area and the Pacific Crest Trail at Dishpan Gap. The trail follows an old logging road for approximately 2.5 miles, traverses an old clear-cut unit, then enters the forest. It eventually opens into Curry Gap, a wide corridor with meadows.

The trail heads south through the gap and eventually reaches a junction. The right fork is the Quartz Creek Trail 1050, which joins the North Fork Skykomish Road 63 on the Skykomish District. The left fork continues further along the ridge with little change in elevation. The trail (almost passing over Bald Eagle, Long John, and June mountains) continues to the Pacific Crest Trail at Dishpan Gap after 9.5 miles.

BEDAL CREEK TRAIL 705

LENGTH: 2.0 miles   BEST SEASONS: summer, fall
LOW ELEVATION: 2800 ft.   HIGH: 4800 ft.   GAIN: 2000 ft.

TRAILHEAD ACCESS 1: From Verlot Public Service Center, travel east on the Mtn. Loop Highway 26 miles to Road 4096. Turn right and continue 2 miles to the trailhead.

TRAILHEAD ACCESS 2: From Darrington Ranger Station, travel south along the Mtn. Loop Highway 20 for 21 miles to Road 4096. Turn left and continue 2 miles to the trailhead.

PARKING AND FACILITIES: Parking available at the trailhead. Parking is limited, so you might want to turn your vehicle around before leaving. Please don't park in the turnaround area.

HENRY M. JACKSON WILDERNESS TRAILS

DESCRIPTION: The trail climbs steadily through thick, old forest punctuated by avalanche chutes before opening into the meadow basin below the steep slopes of Bedal Peak to the left. Massive Sloan Peak towers at the head of the valley. From there the trail gradually disappears into willow, slide alder, brush, and mud before reaching the site of Harry Bedal's trapping cabin or climbers' routes to Bedal and Sloan.

ELLIOTT CREEK (GOAT LAKE) TRAIL 647

LENGTH: 4.5 miles   **BEST SEASONS:** spring, summer, fall
LOW ELEVATION: 1900 ft.   **HIGH:** 3200 ft.   **GAIN:** 1300 ft.

TRAILHEAD ACCESS

Access 1: From the Verlot Public Service Center, travel east on the Mtn. Loop Highway 22.8 miles to the Elliott Creek Road 4080. Turn right and continue 0.8 mile to the trailhead.

Access 2: From Darrington Ranger Station travel south along the Mtn. Loop Highway 20 for 22 miles to the Elliott Creek Road 4080. Turn left and continue 0.8 mile to the trailhead.

PARKING AND FACILITIES: Parking available at trailhead. This is a busy trailhead with limited parking. Please don't park in the turnaround area.

DESCRIPTION: One now has a choice of two trails from the trailhead. Follow the abandoned logging road straight ahead from the trailhead (Goat Lake Trail) or continue 0.25 miles and drop down to the right to Elliot Creek (Elliot Creek Trail) and follow the creek trail (reopened in summer of 1999). Both trails meet up 1.6 miles prior to reaching Goat Lake.

The trail along Elliot Creek enters a beautiful old-growth forest for the first 2 miles. The forest then transforms into second growth timber before rejoining the Goat Lake Trail.

The old logging road/trail is straight forward from the trailhead, initially passing through young alder and hemlock on easy grades. The tread is in good shape with nice views of the valley along the way. After 3.6 miles the trail intersects with the Elliot Creek Trail. In another 0.5 mile you reach the Henry M. Jackson Wilderness Boundary. The last 0.5 mile to Goat Lake consists of steep switchbacks that pass by McIntosh Falls. Please, no camping within 200' of lake shore and no campfires within 0.25 mile of the lake.

GLACIER BASIN TRAIL 719

LENGTH: 2.1 miles **BEST SEASONS:** summer, fall
LOW ELEVATION: 3200 ft. **HIGH:** 4500 ft. **GAIN:** 1300 ft.

TRAILHEAD ACCESS: From the Verlot Public Service Center, travel east on the Mtn. Loop Highway 19.5 miles. Park at Barlow Pass and proceed on foot past the gate at the start of the old Monte Cristo Road. This road is no longer maintained by the County and has received lots of damage over the years. Please note there is no bridge at 1 mile where the road crosses the Sauk River. At mile 4, the road end, cross the bridge over the South Fork Sauk and continue past the cabin area, cross the bridge on the left over 76 Creek and proceed up "Dumas Street" through what was the main street of Monte Cristo to the trailhead at approximately 4.5 miles from Barlow Pass.

PARKING AND FACILITIES: Parking lot at Barlow Pass Trailhead. Toilet, camping, bike racks, and picnic facilities located just prior to Monte Cristo Townsite area.

DESCRIPTION: The trail for the first 0.5 mile follows an old railroad grade, originally established in the 1890s for mining. Then the trail climbs very steeply, more slick rock scramble than hike for a long stretch, past Glacier Falls and the Henry M. Jackson Wilderness Boundary, skirting the northeast edge of Mystery Ridge.

The area is rich in mining history and this heavily visited basin offers exploration, excellent scenery, and climbing for those experienced in mountain climbing and snow travel.

Overnighters are asked to avoid camping in the fragile meadow at the bottom of the basin. There are established campsites on Ray's Knoll and Mystery Ridge. Campfires are prohibited within 0.25 mile of the trail or the Basin Area. Campers should use stoves.

POODLE DOG PASS-SILVER LAKE-TWIN LAKES TRAILS 708

LENGTH: 4.4 miles **BEST SEASONS:** summer, fall
LOW ELEVATION: 2800 ft. **HIGH:** 4800 ft. **GAIN:** 2000 ft.

TRAILHEAD ACCESS: From the Verlot Public Service Center, travel east on the Mtn. Loop Highway for 19.5 miles to Barlow Pass. Park here and proceed on foot past the gate at the start of the old Monte Cristo Road. This road is no longer maintained by the County and has received significant damage over the years. Please note there is no bridge at 1 mile where the road crosses the Sauk River. At mile 4, the road end, cross the bridge over the South Fork Sauk River and continue through the cabin area to two foot bridges. This is the trailhead. Proceed across dry Sunday Creek bed and past the cabin for the start of the trail.

PARKING AND FACILITIES: Parking lot at Barlow Pass Trailhead. Toilet, camping, bike racks, and picnic facilities located just prior to Monte Cristo Townsite area. Backcountry toilets are found at Silver Lake and Twin Lakes.

DESCRIPTION: The trail proceeds upward in long sweeping switchbacks, entering the Henry M. Jackson Wilderness shortly after leaving the cabin area. From here, pass through an open scree field with nice views of the valley and surrounding peaks before descending to Sunday Creek at approximately a mile. From here the trail moves through a boggy area before ascending very steeply up loose scree to Poodle Dog Pass (4350 ft). A short side trail leads to Silver Lake, where there is good camping, a box toilet, but reportedly no fish. Remember to bring a stove as campfires are prohibited here.

Continuing along the main trail, the route climbs and drops steeply again and again, crossing the ridge line several times as it alternately skirts the headwaters of Silver Creek and 76 Creeks. Panoramic views of Wilmans Peak, Columbia Peak and the surrounding ridges can be had at many points along the way. The route includes a rock scramble that holds snow very late in the season. This results in a system of braided, intermittent boot paths that must be navigated with caution. At a bit over two miles that feel like five, come to a splendid viewpoint at 5400 ft. of Twin Lakes 600 feet below. This scenic area offers fishing and exploring; visitors are asked to restrict camping to established sites. Campfires are prohibited within 0.25 mile of Twin Lakes as the use is heavy and down wood is scarce. Find the box toilet off a way trail to the Northeast shortly before reaching the inlet.

SLOAN PEAK TRAIL 648

LENGTH: 4.5 miles   BEST SEASONS: summer, fall
LOW ELEVATION: 1900 ft.   HIGH: 4800 ft.   GAIN: 2900 ft.

TRAILHEAD ACCESS: From Darrington, travel south on the Mtn. Loop Highway 20 for 16.3 miles. Turn left (east) on the Sloan Creek Road 49 and follow it for 4.5 miles to the trailhead on the right.

PARKING AND FACILITIES: Limited parking.

DESCRIPTION: The trail follows an old road for half a mile and then it is necessary to cross the North Fork Sauk River. A foot log that existed for many years has now washed away. Fording the river is possible downstream at low water. This trail receives sporadic maintenance. Be prepared for windfall and brush.

After crossing the river, the trail climbs steeply through timber. It crosses Cougar Creek near a large falls at mile 2.0. This can sometimes be difficult to cross during times of heavy snowmelt. The trail then ascends to the meadows at the base of Sloan Peak.

Hikers without climbing experience should not continue on the trail. The climbing route leads up snow slopes to a ridge overlooking a glacier.

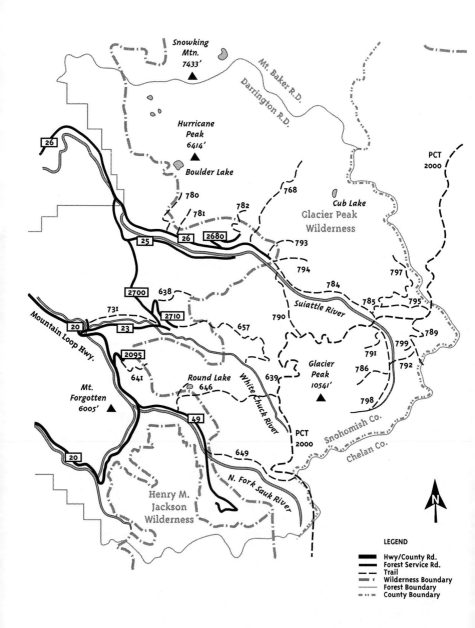

Maps in this trail guide are for general orientation only and are not to scale. Please use a USDA Forest Service or other detailed topographic map for accurate and specific information.

GLACIER PEAK WILDERNESS

The Darrington Ranger District administers 219,767 acres of the Glacier Peak Wilderness. The Glacier Peak Wilderness contains 576,865 acres of land; 35 miles long and 20 miles wide. There are 185 miles of trails on the Darrington District within Glacier Peak Wilderness (369 miles of trails total).

Glacier Peak is the dominant geologic feature of the area and is the most remote of the major volcanic peaks in the Cascade Range. It is 10,541 feet high, the fourth highest peak in Washington. This dormant volcano last erupted 12,000 years ago, spreading ash as far away as eastern Idaho.

Game abounds in the wilderness; one can see deer, mountain goat, black bear, grouse, coyote, and even fox. Smaller animals such as field mice are in constant attendance and are almost certain to visit your camp during the night. Some high mountain lakes can yield good fishing when ice-free, which may not be until August, or not at all in some years.

To help protect wilderness resources and provide you and others with quality wilderness experiences, please familiarize yourself with Leave No Trace, Wilderness Regulations and other information provided in the Introduction to this guide. Campfires are prohibited within 0.25 mile of Image Lake, Lake Byrne and above 4,000 feet elevation along Lime Ridge.

CAMPING IS PROHIBITED IN THE FOLLOWING AREAS:

▸ Image Lake within 0.25 mile of lake: alternate campsites are at the back-packer sites south of the lake and Sunnybrook and Lady Camp. Stock camps are available at Sunnybrook, Lady Camp and near the Miners Cabins as well.

▸ Holden Lake within 200 feet of lake.

▸ Lyman Lake within 200 feet of lake: alternate campsites can be found in the Cloudy Pass area.

GLACIER PEAK WILDERNESS TRAILS

Boulder Lake Trail 740

LENGTH: 2.5 miles   BEST SEASONS: summer, fall
LOW ELEVATION: 3000 ft.   HIGH: 5900 ft.   GAIN: 2000 ft.

TRAILHEAD ACCESS: From Darrington Ranger Station, drive north on Highway 530 seven miles to Forest Service Road 26, on your right just past the bridge over the Sauk River. Follow Road 26 eight miles to the junction with Tenas Creek Road, FS 2660. Drive Tenas Creek Road 7.25 miles to the road end and a parking area on the right.

PARKING AND FACILITIES: Parking area.

DESCRIPTION: This is a steep, rarely maintained trail to a scenic lake popular for fishing. There are several good camp sites for overnight visits.

Find the start of the trail across the road from the parking area as it follows an old road through a logging unit for the first half mile. Enter big timber where the trail has several very steep pitches and portions that are not clearly defined. At 0.75 mile is the boundary of Glacier Peak Wilderness. Soon after the Wilderness boundary the trail trends further upslope away from the creek and leaves timber for open rock and brush with views across to the slopes of Huckleberry Mountain and Hurricane Peak. The trail proceeds north then swings to the east before it crosses the outfall of Boulder Lake and crosses to an abandoned outlet where the trail climbs this steep scramble up to the lake basin. Please tread lightly as this lake is heavily visited and the high walls of the lake cirque create a very short growing season. Use established camp sites and pack out what you packed in. If you choose to have a campfire, use only down and dead wood.

BUCK CREEK PASS TRAIL 789

LENGTH: 5 miles   BEST SEASONS: summer, fall
LOW ELEVATION: 4600 ft.   HIGH: 5900 ft.   GAIN: 300 ft.

TRAILHEAD ACCESS: The trail is within the Glacier Peak Wilderness off of the Pacific Crest Trail 2000, 2.3 miles west from Suiattle Pass and 4.3 miles east from Suiattle River Trail 784.

PARKING AND FACILITIES: See Suiattle Trailhead.

DESCRIPTION: The trail begins climbing out of the valley floor, switchbacking steeply up the hill. At 2 miles Sheep Camp Trail 787 leaves on the left (east). As the name implies, this trail was once heavily used by sheepherders. This short, 1 mile trail follows along a ridge below Fortress Mountain to some views of Glacier Peak. Excellent camp spots here for horsemen and backpackers, since water is available.

After descending continuously, with occasional views to the headwaters of the Suiattle, to Small Creek, and ascending steeply through a brush field, you come to Buck Creek Pass which is famed for its vistas of Glacier Peak. On a clear day, views from Flower Dome, Helmut Butte, and Liberty Cap are among the most magnificent in the wilderness. The pass is closed to horse camping except in designated horse camps.

Flower Dome Trail 799 is 0.5 mile north of the pass. This short, one-mile route follows along a meadow-covered alpine spur to the rounded summit. A hike to the top of this aptly named mountain has views and meadows with a wide selection of wildflowers. Buck Creek Trail 1513 continues for 9.3 miles and ends at Chiwawa River Road 311 on the Wenatchee National Forest.

CANYON LAKE TRAIL 797

〰 🚶

LENGTH: 7 miles   BEST SEASONS: summer, fall
LOW ELEVATION: 5650 ft.   HIGH: 6050 ft.   GAIN: 400 ft.

> **TRAILHEAD ACCESS:** The trail is within the Glacier Peak Wilderness and starts 0.3 mile east of Image Lake.

> **DESCRIPTION:** Leading around the upper basin rim of Image Lake and climbing gradually to the saddle, the trail then drops over heathery knolls, traversing Plummer Mountain. There is often snow here through the summer. Following a flower-covered ridge, the trail contours around to the north and passes just below Sitting Bull Mountain. At 3.5 miles, the trail climbs higher, passing through many heather benches and small streams. This is a delightful stretch of trail. The trail leads down rather steeply for the last mile to 21.3-acre Canyon Lake, elevation 5050 ft., set in a steep-walled basin.

CRYSTAL LAKE TRAIL 638

〰 🚶

LENGTH: 5 miles   BEST SEASONS: summer, fall
LOW ELEVATION: 2500 ft.   HIGH: 4500 ft.   GAIN: 2000 ft.

> **TRAILHEAD ACCESS:** From the Darrington Ranger Station, take Mtn. Loop Highway for 9 miles to White Chuck Road 23 and turn left (east). Follow this road for 6 miles to Rat Trap Pass Road 2700 (signed Meadow Mountain Trail). Turn left (north) and drive 2.4 miles to the trailhead (it may not be signed) on your right. In October, 2003 a devastating flood washed out the Whitechuck Road 23 in several locations. The first washout closes the road at 1.2 miles. It is expected that repairs to the road will take several years or more.

PARKING AND FACILITIES: Limited parking at trailhead. Backcountry toilet at lake.

DESCRIPTION: Follow Trail 657 (Meadow Mountain Trail) for approximately 1.5 miles to a junction. Go left on Crystal Lake Trail 638. After 2 miles past the junction the trail gets much steeper and follows an old fire line bordering an old clear-cut. Just above where the fire line meets the old trail find Trail 638.1 which traverses 2.5 miles through big timber, up and over Scar Pass, through an old logging unit, a series of huckleberry filled meadows and onward to Circle Peak. The last 200 yards to the old lookout site is for the more experienced scrambler. The trail then enters old-growth forest for the last 0.5 mile and comes out at 20.8-acre Crystal Lake, elevation 4800 ft. There are numerous camp spots nestled among the trees. Please camp at established sites.

DOWNEY CREEK TRAIL 768

LENGTH: 6.6 miles BEST SEASONS: spring, summer, fall
LOW ELEVATION: 1400 ft. HIGH: 2400 ft. GAIN: 1000 ft.

TRAILHEAD ACCESS: From the Darrington Ranger Station, drive north 7 miles to Suiattle River Road 26. Follow this road east for 20 miles to Downey Creek Campground. The trail is just past the Downey Creek Bridge on the left (north) side of the road. The Suiattle River Road 26 was washed out in the 2003 and 2006 floods; repairs are expected to begin in late 2010. Contact the Darrington Ranger District for updates.

PARKING AND FACILITIES: Parking lot and toilet facilities at trailhead.

DESCRIPTION: The trail climbs steadily, winding in and out among tall trees for the first mile. This trail is affected by many small springs feeding Downey Creek. The trail follows close to the creek and a pleasant camp spot is located at 3 miles. The trail ends at Bachelor Creek at 6.6 miles where there are a couple of camp sites.

GREEN MOUNTAIN TRAIL 782

LENGTH: 4 miles BEST SEASONS: summer, fall
LOW ELEVATION: 3500 ft. HIGH: 6500 ft. GAIN: 3000 ft.

TRAILHEAD ACCESS: From the Darrington Ranger Station drive north 7 miles to the Suiattle River Road 26. Follow this road 20.2 miles to Road 2680 on the left (north). Drive for 5.9 miles to the trailhead where parking is available. The Suiattle River Road 26 was washed out in the 2003 and 2006 floods; repairs are expected in late 2010. Contact the Darrington Ranger District for updates.

PARKING AND FACILITIES: Small parking lot at trailhead. A backcountry toilet is located at the camping area at 2.5 miles, east and down from the trail near a small tarn.

DESCRIPTION: The trail climbs rather steeply through old-growth timber for the first mile before breaking out into the large meadows, which give the mountain its name. By July, the meadows are alive with every kind of flower imaginable, making it one of the loveliest trails in the North Cascades.

Please camp only at existing sites designated by fire rings and located below the lakes. The last mile is steep, with switchbacks. Marmots live on these high grassy slopes, and send out their alarm whistle, warning other marmots of your presence.

The lookout, built in 1933, is listed in the National Register of Historic Places. On a clear day, the view from the top is breathtaking: north past Mt. Baker into Canada; east across to Glacier Peak; to the south a string of snowcapped giants; west to Puget Sound.

HUCKLEBERRY MOUNTAIN TRAIL 780

LENGTH: 7 miles   **BEST SEASONS:** spring, summer, fall,
LOW ELEVATION: 1000 ft.   **HIGH:** 5900 ft.   **GAIN:** 4900 ft.

TRAILHEAD ACCESS: From the Darrington Ranger Station, drive north 7 miles to the Suiattle River Road 26. Follow this road for 14.5 miles. The trailhead is on the left (north) and is signed. The Suiattle River Road 26 was washed out in the 2003 and 2006 floods; repairs are expected in late 2010. Contact the Darrington Ranger District for updates.

PARKING AND FACILITIES: There is a parking lot at the trailhead.

DESCRIPTION: The trail consists of numerous switchbacks which climb steeply up the mountain. Small cascading waterfalls from many streams can be seen along the way, making this an enjoyable hike. A camping spot near a stream is located at 4 miles. Since the trail winds up the mountain and passes through timber, there is not much of a view until reaching the top. From the top, the vistas are spectacular—looking east to Glacier Peak, north to Mt. Baker, and south to Whitehorse, Three Fingers, and Mt. Pugh.

KENNEDY RIDGE TRAIL 639

LENGTH: 2 miles   **BEST SEASONS:** summer, fall
LOW ELEVATION: 3725 ft.   **HIGH:** 4150 ft.   **GAIN:** 425 ft.

TRAILHEAD ACCESS: Trail is within the Glacier Peak Wilderness. The Kennedy Ridge Trail meets the Pacific Crest National Scenic Trail 2000 (PCT) 0.25 mile north of Kennedy Creek.

DESCRIPTION: Passing through mossy forest along the spine of the ridge with views of Glacier Peak, the trail then switchbacks down to the former site of Kennedy Hot Springs. For off-trail adventurers, a loop can be made through the silt and rubble flats left by the October, 2003 floods that buried the hot springs, across Kennedy Creek, returning to the PCT via the Upper White Chuck Trail 643A. (See Upper White Chuck Trail.)

LENGTH: 11 miles   BEST SEASONS: summer, fall
LOW ELEVATION: 1800 ft.   HIGH: 5700 ft.   GAIN: 3900 ft.

TRAILHEAD ACCESS: From the Darrington Ranger Station, take the Mtn. Loop Highway 20 south along the west side of the Sauk River. Drive 19.7 miles to Sloan Creek Road 49 and turn left. Continue east on road 3.5 miles to the trailhead.

PARKING AND FACILITIES: There is limited parking available.

DESCRIPTION: Be sure to carry water on this route, you can't be sure that water will be found along the way. The trail climbs steeply through open woods for 3 miles to Bingley Gap at 4425 ft.

The route enters Glacier Peak Wilderness and continues climbing up along the ridge to meadows and a saddle overlooking 12.0-acre Round Lake, at 5100 ft. No stock animals are allowed beyond this point. A 0.7 mile side trail drops down to the lake. Camp spots can be found here among the trees. The main trail continues past 0.5-acre Sun-Up Lake at 5300 ft. The trail becomes harder to follow. Hikers must follow boot tread, blazes, and cross-country travel. Early season travel can be hazardous because of high-angle snow slopes and difficult route finding. Following the ridge, passing through vast meadows and through open basins with constantly changing views, the trail passes 0.7-acre Hardtack Lake at 5450 ft. and at 11 miles it reaches 9.9-acre Camp Lake at 5700 ft. From here the Lost Creek Ridge Trail climbs to a knoll, then drops to a rocky basin and descends to 51.2-acre Lake Byrne at 5550 ft. The trail then descends 2250 ft. for 2 miles to the former Kennedy Hot Springs and the junction with the White Chuck Trail 643. Floods in October 2003 washed out bridges over the White Chuck River and Kennedy Creek. Fording the Whitechuck River is extremely dangerous and not recommended at any time of year. Access to the White Chuck area and Pacific Crest National Scenic Trail via Lost Creek Ridge Trail is not recommended.

MEADOW MOUNTAIN TRAIL 657

LENGTH: 17.5 miles   BEST SEASONS: summer, fall
LOW ELEVATION: 2500 ft.   HIGH: 5850 ft.   GAIN: 3350 ft.

TRAILHEAD ACCESS: From the Darrington Ranger Station, take the Mtn. Loop Highway 9 miles to the White Chuck Road 23 and turn left (east). Follow this road for 6 miles to the Rat Trap Pass Road 2700 (signed Meadow Mountain Trail). Turn left (north) and drive 2.4 miles to the trailhead (may not be signed) on your right. In October, 2003 a devastating flood washed out the Whitechuck Road 23 in several locations. The first washout closes the road at 1.2 miles. It is expected that repairs to the road will take several years or more.

PARKING AND FACILITIES: Limited parking at trailhead.

DESCRIPTION: This trail begins on an old road which climbs steadily and then drops to a junction with the Crystal Lake Trail. Stay right and continue another four miles to the former road end where the trail takes off to your left and climbs steeply through dense woods before reaching the first meadow. A small stream nearby suggests a relaxing pause for lunch. The trail continues on for another 1.5 miles until the junction with the Meadow Lake Trail 657A on the left (east). Drop down 0.7 mile to the 11-acre lake, which is in a beautiful alpine setting, cliffs on one side, trees and meadows on the other. The main trail continues on past the lake turnoff, angling up a ridge passing forest and meadows at 2 miles.

The fall colors of these meadows and ripe blueberries in September and October are well worth the effort involved to visit the areas.

The trail continues going up and down, gaining and losing elevation, with numerous switchbacks and always excellent views of Glacier Peak. Although camp spots are frequent along the way, the first site with guaranteed water is at 8.5 miles. The ridge crest is neared at 5850 ft. From here, 9.6-acre Diamond Lake at 5250 ft. and 11-acre Emerald Lake at 5150 ft. are accessible by compass and map only, since there is not a trail to either lake. The trail continues up and down along the ridge and proceeds through patches of trees, flowers, and fantastic views, eventually dropping down with a few switchbacks. Campsites are available along the trail. At 12 miles the trail passes by Fire Mountain. Hikers can continue from here to the junction with the former White Chuck Trail, which was obliterated in the 2003 floods.

MILK CREEK TRAIL 790

LENGTH: 5.5 miles   BEST SEASONS: summer, fall
LOW ELEVATION: 1650 ft.   HIGH: 4000 ft.   GAIN: 2350 ft.

TRAILHEAD ACCESS: From Darrington Ranger Station, drive north 7 miles to the Suiattle River Road 26. Follow this road for 23 miles to the road end. The Suiattle River Road 26 was washed out in the 2003 and 2006 floods; repairs are expected to begin in late 2010. Contact the Darrington Ranger District for updates. Follow the Suiattle River Trail 784 past the wilderness boundary for 1 mile. The Milk Creek Trail is on the right. There is no bridge access from the Suiattle River Trail. Fording the Suiattle River is extremely dangerous and not recommended any time of the year. The trail is best accessed from the Pacific Crest Trail. This trail is not currently maintained.

PARKING AND FACILITIES: Stock facilities, stock camp at Suiattle River Trailhead. Parking lot and toilet facilities at Suiattle Trailhead.

DESCRIPTION: The Milk Creek trail has not been maintained since 2003. Expect windfall, severe brush, and route finding challenges. Please note that there is no bridge crossing the Suiattle River.

The trail begins in a grove of ancient trees, climbing gradually to enter the Milk Creek Valley. The route winds through a dark rain forest and crosses numerous streams. There are campsites at the 3.0 milepost near the first crossing of Milk Creek, and at approximately the 4.5 milepost and 5.5 milepost. Following a gentle slope, the trail then begins climbing across brush fields, and ending at the junction with the Pacific Crest Trail 2000.

LENGTH: 9.9 miles   BEST SEASONS: summer, fall
LOW ELEVATION: 2900 ft.   HIGH: 5500 ft.   GAIN: 2600 ft.

TRAILHEAD ACCESS: Follow the Suiattle River for 9.3 miles. The trail is on the left (north) and is signed.

PARKING AND FACILITIES: Parking facilities at Suiattle Trailhead. See below for camping options.

DESCRIPTION: Be sure to fill canteens before leaving the Suiattle River Trail because there is not a dependable source of water along the trail. This trail starts quickly and relentlessly switchbacking through open forest with occasional glimpses of the valley below.

A junction at 3.2 miles provides a pleasant camp spot on the side of the trail called Sunnybrook Camp. The trail straight ahead, Miners Cabin Trail 795, leads to Suiattle Pass, traversing the hillside below Miners Ridge and ending at the Glacier Peak Mines after 2 miles. Miners Ridge Trail is the left (north) fork. Switchbacking up through meadows and forest the trail reaches the ridge at 2.3 miles and another junction. To the left 0.3 mile is Miners Ridge Lookout at 6210 ft., built in 1938 and rebuilt in 1952. The lookout is used today by wilderness rangers stationed there during the summer.

The main trail turns right (east) 0.7 mile traversing the hillside to 3.8-acre Image Lake at 6050 ft. Stock users are asked to use the horse trail through the basin. A hitching area is provided near the Canyon Lake Trail junction at the east rim of the lake basin so that riders can enjoy day use of the lake. Horse camping is available 1 mile east of the lake at Lady Camp. Backpackers may camp in the area just southeast of the lake. Camping elsewhere in the lake basin is prohibited. Campfires are prohibited within 0.25 mile of the lake as down and dead wood is very scarce in this popular high alpine area.

Some people consider Miners Ridge to be one of the most beautiful places in the wilderness. From Image Lake toward Suiattle Pass, hikers are afforded views of Glacier Peak, Plummer Mountain, North Star, and Fortress Mountain. Wildflower displays are abundant in mid-July and August.

The junction with the Miners Cabin Trail 795 is at Glacier Peak Mines, 1.4 miles east of Image Lake. The Miners Ridge Trail traverses the hillside for another 1.6 miles where it joins the PCT 2000 at 0.7 mile west of Suiattle Pass.

MT. PUGH TRAIL 644

LENGTH: 3.5 miles   BEST SEASONS: summer, fall
LOW ELEVATION: 1900 ft.   HIGH: 5000 ft.   GAIN: 3100 ft.

TRAILHEAD ACCESS: From the Darrington Ranger Station, drive the Mtn. Loop Highway 20 for 14 miles to Road 2095 on your left (east) and proceed for 1 mile. The trailhead is on your right and should be signed.

PARKING AND FACILITIES: Limited parking at trailhead.

DESCRIPTION: The trail climbs steeply through deep forest for 1.5 miles before reaching Lake Metan, at 2800 ft. Just before the lake, there is a spring and the last chance for water before proceeding on the trail. The trail continues with long gradual switchbacks ascending to a small meadow at 3.5 miles.

Mountain goats can frequently be seen on the upper slopes of the drainage. From here the trail becomes steeper and continues with switchbacks until you come out at timberline at Stujack Pass. Excellent views can be enjoyed here. Hikers without climbing experience should not continue on. The footpath treads over a razorback ridge to the top. In places the trail has been blasted out of rock. You should be equipped for steep snow travel during early summer, and for rock scrambling all summer.

A lookout was built on Mt. Pugh in 1927, but has long since been destroyed. You might see remnants of a tramway used to haul building materials to the top. Views from the top are magnificent. All of the Cascades are visible on a clear day—from Mt. Baker and Mt. Rainier to Glacier Peak.

NORTH FORK SAUK TRAIL 649

LENGTH: 8.4 miles   BEST SEASONS: summer, fall
LOW ELEVATION: 2100 ft.   HIGH: 6000 ft.   GAIN: 3900 ft.

TRAILHEAD ACCESS:

Access 1: From the Darrington Ranger Station, take Mtn. Loop Highway 20 along the west side of the Sauk River. Drive 19.7 miles to the Sloan Creek Road 49 and turn left. Drive that road 6.6 miles to the trailhead.

Access 2: From the Verlot Public Service Center, drive east along the Mtn. Loop Highway to Sloan Creek Road 49 and turn right. Drive that road 6.6 miles to the trailhead.

PARKING AND FACILITIES: Parking lot with stock vehicle parking and unloading ramp, stock campground, corral, and toilet facilities at trailhead.

DESCRIPTION: This trail begins in an old-growth forest and enters Glacier Peak Wilderness at 0.5 mile. Climbing gradually, the trail passes through a magnificent cedar forest and occasional avalanche swaths. Campsites can be found in 3.5 miles at 2800 ft. and at 5 miles at Mackinaw Shelter at 2950 ft.

From here the trail begins climbing with relentless switchbacks gaining 3000 ft. in 3 miles. The switchbacks seem unending, but scenic vistas begin and improve as altitude is gained. The alpine meadows and the splendid view make it well worth the effort. At 8.4 miles the trail reaches the PCT 2000. From here hikers may go north on the PCT to Red Pass and beyond, or make a loop by taking the PCT south, traveling 6.5 miles to Dishpan Gap, then 11 miles on the Pilot Ridge Trail 652, returning to the North Fork Sauk Trail. The total length of this hike would be 26 miles. See Pilot Ridge Trail 652 for further information.

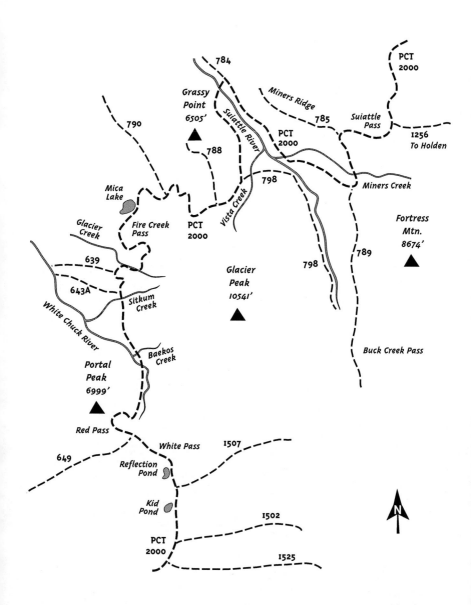

Maps in this trail guide are for general orientation only and are not to scale. Please use a USDA Forest Service or other detailed topographic map for accurate and specific information.

PACIFIC CREST TRAIL INFORMATION

▶ No telephones: to reach the nearest phones travel from North Fork Sauk trailhead to Darrington (24 miles), from Suiattle trailhead to Darrington (28 miles).

▶ Infrequent water: Reflection Pond to Glacier Peak Meadows (1 mile north of Red Pass).

▶ No Post Office facilities: nearest post office in Darrington.

▶ Trailheads with stock facilities:

North Fork Sauk: water, loading ramp, corral

Suiattle: water, loading ramp

▶ Developed campgrounds: Sulphur Creek (0.25 mile east of Suiattle trailhead); stock camps at North Fork Sauk and Suiattle.

▶ Limited grazing: Glacier Peak Meadows, 1 mile north of Red Pass, to Glacier Creek, approximately 12 miles; East Fork Basin, Vista Ridge to Suiattle Pass approximately 15 miles.

▶ Please do not camp at:

White Pass (camp south on a bench below the pass or north in Foam Basin)

Red Pass (camp northeast in Glacier Peak Meadows)

Suiattle Pass (camp south or west of pass)

PACIFIC CREST NATIONAL SCENIC TRAIL 2000 (PCT)

🏞 🧍 🐴 🐕

LENGTH: 45 miles **BEST SEASONS:** summer, fall
LOW ELEVATION: 2800 ft. **(Suiattle River Crossing)**
HIGH: 6450 ft. **(Red Pass)** **GAIN:** 3650 ft.

TRAILHEAD ACCESS: The Pacific Crest National Scenic Trail (PCT) on the Darrington District is accessed via the North Fork Sauk and Suiattle River Trails. Please see these trails for parking and facilities information.

DESCRIPTION: The segment of the PCT administered by the Darrington Ranger District is described here beginning from the junction of the Little Wenatchee Trail 1525 at the south end of the district heading north to Suiattle Pass. From Little Wenatchee Trail 1525 junction the tail follows broad, intermittently meadow covered ridges 2.3 miles to the Indian Creek Trail 1502 junction. There are established camp sites and a box toilet in the broad expanse of low meadow known as Indian Pass.

From Indian Pass the trail gains gradually, passing a small tarn called Kid Pond (5300 ft.) and reaching the White River Trail 1507 at 4 miles. Just north of this junction is Reflection Pond where there is an established camp. Here the trail leaves tree line for open meadowlands and expansive views, reaching White Pass at 5904 ft. Please do not camp next to the trail in the White Pass area as the area has been excessively impacted by camping. A better camp was created 75 feet below the pass itself on a bench to the southwest. A box toilet is provided. There are magnificent views of Sloan Peak and the Monte Cristo range from here. Dry years may require a short walk into Foam Basin for water.

The trail swings to the west here, traversing steadily upward across open slopes and through rocky draws which can hold steep snow until late in the season, passing the junction of the North Fork Sauk Trail 649 at 6.5 miles. This is the last exit from the PCT until reaching the Suiattle River Trail 32 miles to the north.

Continue upward toward Red Pass (6450 ft.), a narrow pass south of Portal Peak. Please do not camp at Red Pass. It is a small area and the vegetation is extremely fragile. The trail descends from here through scree, stonecrop and scattered heather to excellent camping in the grassy meadows below known as Glacier Peak Meadows at approximately 5700 feet. There are many sites here with stunning views of Glacier Peak and the surroundings. There is consistent water and a box toilet is provided.

Leaving Glacier Peak meadows, the trail descends through parkland areas and into big timber as it switchbacks down to the crossing of the White Chuck River and a dramatic view of the head waters surging through this narrow gorge. The trail continues mostly in forest as it passes over a series of relatively flat benches. Hikers will encounter evidence of the torrential flood of 2003 at Baekos creek and glimpse brief views of remote Black Mountain (7262 ft.) across from Chetwot meadows. Approximately 7 miles after leaving Glacier Peak Meadows find the intersection with the upper

White Chuck Trail 643A which descends to the confluence of Kennedy Creek and the White Chuck River, former site of Kennedy Hot Springs. There are no remaining campsites or bridges. Future reconstruction may allow trail re-connection to Lost Creek Ridge and Kennedy Ridge trails.

From the Upper White Chuck Trail 643A, the PCT descends steeply into the Kennedy Creek drainage before crossing Kennedy Creek. Shortly afterward is the junction with Kennedy Ridge Trail 639. The PCT then climbs steadily following an old moraine coming out of forest at Glacier Creek where good camps and a box toilet can be found. From here the trail continues upward, crossing the nose of a ridge into Pumice Creek Basin and vast open meadows and good camping. Once past Pumice Creek, the trail drops and climbs as it passes through a number of small basins before reaching the last camp before Fire Creek Pass at 1.5 miles. From here the trail switchbacks up to 6300 foot Fire Creek Pass. The north side of the pass holds snow late, often into late July or August, making the descent treacherous.

From the pass, continue down 1.5 miles to Mica Lake. It's a picturesque 5-acre lake at 5500 feet, often enshrouded in snow until late in the season. Good camping and a box toilet are 0.5 mile north of Mica lake at Mica Meadows. It is better to camp here rather than at Milk Creek, where there are no campsites.

From Mica Meadows switchbacks lead down to Milk Creek at 4000 ft. After crossing Milk Creek, there is a junction for Milk Creek Trail 790. This trail has not been maintained since before the 2003 floods which removed the bridge over the Suiattle River. This trail is a remote backcountry descent, past brushy meadows, good camps and ancient forest ending at the river. Milk Creek Trail 790 is not a viable way to exit from the PCT.

The PCT switchbacks up the east wall of the canyon and approximately 5300 ft. reaches a ridge crest. Campsites can be found along this stretch, however water may only be available at East Fork Creek late in the season. On the west end of the basin, the PCT crosses a ridge and the junction with Grassy Point Trail 788. This rarely maintained 2.8 mile spur trail runs north from the PCT passing through numerous grassy meadows as it climbs to 6505 ft. at Grassy Point. There is limited water. The PCT continues along Vista Ridge where a few campsites can be found. The mountain views and wildflowers are superb but water can be scarce in summer. From the ridge the trail switchbacks down into Vista Creek and a camp spot near water.

At Vista Creek the trail has been rerouted to a new crossing of the Suiattle River. The new PCT location to be constructed in 2010 winds downstream through 3 miles of old growth forest before crossing the Suiattle River just above Canyon Creek. This is the new junction of the PCT with the Suiattle River Trail. The PCT then continues east approximately 3 miles before reaching the junction with Miners Ridge Trail 795. In another 1.4 miles the trail begins the 8.4 mile climb to Suiattle Pass, 5983 ft. A campsite at Miners Creek, a grassy camp just before the pass and the rolling parklands west of the pass reached by a long spur trail afford the best camping. The Chelan Ranger District on the Wenatchee National Forest administers the PCT from this point northward.

PILOT RIDGE TRAIL 652

LENGTH: 11 miles   BEST SEASONS: summer, fall
LOW ELEVATION: 2450 ft.   HIGH: 5946 ft.   GAIN: 3496 ft.

TRAILHEAD ACCESS

Access 1: From the Darrington Ranger Station, take the Mtn. Loop Highway 20 south along the west side of the Sauk River. Drive 19.7 miles to Sloan Creek Road 49 and turn left (east). Drive this road for 6.6 miles to the North Fork Sauk Trailhead.

Access 2: From the Verlot Public Service Center, drive Mtn. Loop Highway east 27 miles to Sloan Creek Road 49. Turn right (east) and drive this road for 6.6 miles to the trailhead.

Note: The Pilot Ridge Trail is difficult for pack and saddle stock because the narrow trail, out sloping rock, and high rocky steps present hazards to the most experienced stock handler.

PARKING AND FACILITIES: Parking, camp, and toilet facilities available at the North Fork Sauk Trailhead.

DESCRIPTION: Follow the North Fork Sauk Trail 649 for 2 miles; turn right (south) at the junction, crossing the North Fork Sauk River. There is no bridge here and the crossing can be very difficult. This is also the last year round water source until Blue Lakes.

The trail continues for 3 miles, gaining 3000 ft. in a series of switchbacks. The trail follows the ridge before coming out of the trees and into meadows.

On a clear day the view from the ridge is very rewarding; looking south to the Monte Cristo Peaks, Mt. Rainier, and east to Glacier Peak.

At 10 miles a side trail to the east climbs for 1 mile to the 6712 ft. summit of Johnson Mountain. The main trail reaches a junction at 10.5 miles. The left fork leads to cliff-walled, 22-acre Upper Blue Lake at 5500 ft. which may remain frozen until mid-August. The right fork leads to 3-acre Lower Blue Lake in 0.5 mile.

The right fork is the main trail, which ends at June Mountain at a junction with the Bald Eagle Trail 650. The Bald Eagle Trail can be followed east for 2.5 miles to Dishpan Gap at the junction with the PCT 2000.

Make a loop trip by traveling north 6.5 miles on the PCT, through Indian Pass and White Pass, and traveling 8.5 miles down the North Fork Sauk Trail 649. The total length of the loop trip is 26 miles.

See North Fork Sauk Trail 649 for further information regarding that trail.

LENGTH: 0.9 mile   **BEST SEASONS:** summer, fall
LOW ELEVATION: 2100 ft.   **HIGH:** 2800 ft.   **GAIN:** 700 ft.

TRAILHEAD ACCESS: From Darrington Ranger Station, follow Mtn. Loop Highway 20 for 19.7 miles to Sloan Creek Road 49 and turn left. Follow this road for 6.6 miles to the parking area located just off Road 49. The trail for Red Mountain is 100 yards in from there.

PARKING AND FACILITIES: See North Fork Sauk Trailhead.

DESCRIPTION: This seldom-used trail leads through an old-growth forest with magnificent, large trees to the site of an old fire lookout built in the 1930s. Some of the firs in the deep forest on both sides of the trail measure six feet thick at their base.

The old lookout site has excellent views of the Pride Basin glaciers and land to the south. The trail ends at a rock outcropping a short distance beyond the lookout.

SUIATTLE RIVER TRAIL 784

LENGTH: 6.5 miles   **BEST SEASONS:** spring, summer, fall
LOW ELEVATION: 1600 ft.   **HIGH:** 2800 ft.   **GAIN:** 1200 ft.

TRAILHEAD ACCESS: From Darrington Ranger Station, drive north on the highway toward Rockport, 7 miles to the Suiattle River Road 26. Follow this road 22.6 miles to the end of the road. The Suiattle River Road 26 was washed out in the 2003 and 2006 floods; repairs are expected to start in late 2010. Contact the Darrington Ranger District for updates.

PARKING AND FACILITIES: Parking lot with stock vehicle parking and unloading ramp, stock campground, corral and toilet facilities at trailhead.

DESCRIPTION: Follow an abandoned road past the wilderness boundary and proceed for 1 mile to the junction with the Milk Creek Trail 790. The Suiattle River Trail is on the left (east).

As the trail winds in and out of stream gullies, maintaining a fairly level grade, it passes through groves of old and young trees for 5.8 miles to Canyon Creek. There are many camp sites here and a box toilet. Just beyond is the new junction with the Pacific Crest Trail; turn south to cross the Suiattle River or north to head toward Miners Ridge and Suiattle Pass.

SULPHUR CREEK TRAIL 793

LENGTH: 1.8 miles   BEST SEASONS: spring, summer, fall
LOW ELEVATION: 1500 ft.   HIGH: 2040 ft.   GAIN: 540 ft.

TRAILHEAD ACCESS: From Darrington Ranger Station, drive north 7 miles to Suiattle River Road 26. Follow this road 21.5 miles to the Sulphur Creek Campground. The trail is on the left (north) across from the campground. The Suiattle River Road 26 was washed out in the 2003 and 2006 floods; repairs are expected in late 2010. Contact the Darrington Ranger District for updates

PARKING AND FACILITIES: Limited parking.

DESCRIPTION: This trail climbs steeply at first, traveling through a forest of young and old-growth timber. The route follows the creek, winding in and out high above the water. It eventually drops down to follow the creek more closely, passing small pools and waterfalls.

SULPHUR MOUNTAIN TRAIL 794

LENGTH: 5 miles   BEST SEASONS: summer, fall
LOW ELEVATION: 1800 ft.   HIGH: 6000 ft.   GAIN: 4200 ft.

TRAILHEAD ACCESS: From Darrington Ranger Station, drive north 7 miles to the Suiattle River Road 26. Follow this road to the end for 22.6 miles. The trail is 0.1 mile from the end of the road off of the Suiattle River Trail 784. The Suiattle River Road 26 was washed out in the 2003 and 2006 floods; repairs are expected in late 2010. Contact the Darrington Ranger District for updates

PARKING AND FACILITIES: See Suiattle River Trailhead.

DESCRIPTION: The trail begins switchbacking steeply and travels through timbered thickets. A small stream at 1 mile is the last chance for water.

A semi-open hillside provides glimpses of the peaks above Milk Creek at 3 miles. Following a ridge crest for a short way, the trail crosses a meadow and offers a view of Glacier Peak.

The trail reaches the meadow-covered ridge. It is well worth the effort, for the views are impressive. Camping is available here, but there is no water.

TRAILHEAD ACCESS: The Upper White Chuck Trail meets the Pacific Crest National Scenic Trail 2000 (PCT) 0.25 mile north of Sitkum Creek.

DESCRIPTION: From the junction with the PCT 0.25 mile north of Sitkum Creek, the Upper White Chuck trail descends to the former site of Kennedy Hot Springs, where silty Kennedy Creek joins the clear waters of the White Chuck River.

The October 2003 flood dramatically changed the landscape around the hot springs area. The hot springs are now covered under a deep layer of silt and boulders, and Kennedy Cabin was swept downstream along with all the bridges in the area. The former White Chuck Trail washed out in numerous locations and over half its former 5 mile length is completely gone. Hikers should consider this area an off trail adventure for experienced route finders only.

TRAIL INDEX

TRAIL NAME	TRAIL NUMBER	PAGE
NON-WILDERNESS TRAILS		
Ashland Lakes Trail	DNR	10
Bald Mountain Trail	DNR	11
Barlow Point Trail	709	11
Bear Lake Trail	661	12
Beaver Lake Trail	783	12
Big Four Ice Caves Trail	723	13
Boardman Lake and Lake Evan Trail	704	13
Chockwich Mtn. Bike Trail	647.2	14
Coal Lake Trail	632	15
Forks of Canyon Creek Trail	633	15
Frog Lake Trail	659	15
Harold Engles Memorial Grove Trail	642	16
Heather Lake Trail	701	16
Independence Lake Trail	712	17
Lake Twenty-Two Trail	702	17
Lookout Tree Trail	783.1	18
Mallardy Ridge (Walt Bailey's Trail)	706	18
Mt. Dickerman Trail	710	19
Mt. Forgotten Meadows (Perry Creek Trail)	711	19
Mt. Higgins Trail	640	20
Mount Pilchuck Lookout Trail	700	20
North Fork Sauk Falls	660	21
North Lake Trail	712	21
Old Government Trail	733	22
Old Sauk Trail	728	22
Peek-A-Boo Lake Trail	656	23
Pinnacle Lake Trail	703	23
Sunrise Mine Trail	707	23
Weden Creek (Gothic Basin) Trail	724	24
White Chuck Bench Trail	731	25
Youth On Age	738	25

TRAIL NAME	TRAIL NUMBER	PAGE
BOULDER RIVER WILDERNESS TRAILS		
Boulder River Trail	734	27
Deer Creek Pass Trail	717	28
Eight-Mile Trail	654.1	28
Goat Flat-Saddle Lake-Three Fingers	641	28
Kelcema Lake	718	29
Marten Creek Trail	713	29
Niederprum Trail (Whitehorse)	653	30
Squire Creek Trail	654	30
HENRY M. JACKSON WILDERNESS TRAILS		
Bald Eagle (Curry Gap) Trail	650	34
Bedal Creek Trail	705	34
Elliott Creek (Goat Lake) Trail	647	35
Glacier Basin Trail	719	36
Poodle Dog Pass-Silver Lake-Twin Lakes Trails	708	36
Sloan Peak Trail	648	37
GLACIER PEAK WILDERNESS TRAILS		
Boulder Lake Trail	740	43
Buck Creek Trail	789	43
Canyon Lake Trail	797	44
Crystal Lake Trail	638	44
Downey Creek Trail	768	45
Green Mountain Trail	782	45
Huckleberry Mountain Trail	780	46
Kennedy Ridge Trail	639	46
Lost Creek Ridge Trail	646	47
Meadow Mountain Trail	657	47
Milk Creek Trail	790	48
Miners Ridge Trail	785	49
Mt. Pugh Trail	644	49
North Fork Sauk Trail	649	50
Pacific Crest Trail	2000	54

TRAIL NAME	TRAIL NUMBER	PAGE
PACIFIC CREST TRAIL		
Pilot Ridge Trail	652	56
Red Mountain Trail	651	57
Suiattle River Trail	784	57
Sulphur Creek Trail	793	58
Sulphur Mountain Trail	794	58
White Chuck Trail	643A	59